Do Cows Moo On The Other Side?

Do Cows Moo On The Other Side?

Life in the Spirit World

The Rev. Sarah Eagle, U.C.M.

Writers Club Press
San Jose New York Lincoln Shanghai

Do Cows Moo On The Other Side?
Life in the Spirit World

Writers Club Press
an imprint of iUniverse, Inc.

For information address:
iUniverse, Inc.
5220 S. 16th St., Suite 200
Lincoln, NE 68512
www.iuniverse.com

ISBN: 0-595-22224-2

Printed in the United States of America

To my two beautiful families—Spirit and Earth

Contents

Foreword ix

Preface xv

Conversations with My Friends

The Conversations Begin 3

Epilogue 109

Notes 113

Foreword

Where is the Spirit World? Where are we going when we leave this Earth? Heaven, with streets paved in gold and winged angels on white clouds playing harps? The Other Place, with fire and brimstone? Another planet? Nowhere?

None of the above, according to my Spirit family, with whom I frequently communicate. They are: Richard, my Spirit guide, a famous artist who left this earth over fifty years ago, my five wonderful angels, and a mischievous feline-loving sprite/Spirit who invaded my house and behaves only if he has a cat to play with. They are not what you might expect of Spirit beings, but I think you will love them all.

I never thought of writing a book. This was Richard's bright idea, and, as you will learn, he is a very determined entity. What Richard wants, Richard gets. Actually, his desire is to document our communications and share our beautiful story with the world. I am delighted to introduce my Spirit family and the world they live in.

I. The Angels

Edelweiss—the "boss" angel. She has Earth experience as an invisible observer. She knows all of our mortal customs and speech habits, even slang. You might say she is "street wise!" Her sharp sense of humor and down-to-earth approach to life both on earth and in Spirit must have been a plus in her learning experience here. The angels have never given me their descriptions, but I visualize Edelweiss with silver-white hair and amber eyes, the colors of her namesake flower that grows and blooms high in the Alps. She wears a soft, loose green robe the shade of mountain grass. Edelweiss wears no shoes. Would you believe a toe ring, in the shape of a tiny white flower?

Edelweiss is gentle, but tough. She has great powers and the wisdom to generate them effectively. She says angels get around very well without wings—that "we only pose with them for pictures!" She was appointed by higher angels for my welfare when I prayed fervently for guidance, and it was she who chose the other four angels to complete my sweet, beautiful, gentle, and powerful angel band.

Rainbow. One of the most beloved beings in the Spirit world. She oversees welcoming and caring for children arriving in their new world and is in charge of their education. She teaches them art, their favorite subject. We will learn more about these beautiful children and their happy existence in a later chapter.

Rainbow brings peace and beauty following rainstorms, and can even avert bad weather. Thanks to her intervention, not one of the violent storms of 1999 and 2000 hit this area. Rainbow has long, golden-red hair and bright blue eyes. Her flowing robe is of all colors of the glowing arc that brightens the sky and brings hope for a new beginning.

Dewdrop. During the might I rest peacefully, knowing she is guarding my home, my pet, and me. At dawn she brings freshness to Earth in her caress. Her twinkle in the early morning sun forecasts a beautiful day. During a bad drought recently, which everyone feared would last another two months, I joined with many others in praying for rain. Almost immediately the forecasts changed and showers were soaking the dry ground to relieve our arid existence. The trees in a nearby orange grove that had lost their blooms sprouted new ones.

Dewdrop's dark African features represent the beauty of night, and her sarong of sky-blue a lovely new day. She wears silver flats on her tiny feet.

Because she and her sister angel Rosebud love to keep up with events both on earth and in Spirit, they were assigned what Edelweiss calls the "news media" and keep everyone in their community advised accordingly. Richard and the other Spirits tease them about being gossips. Politics, weather, sports, movies, TV and all the entertainment world (including soap operas), war, scandals, name it—they don't miss a thing.

Snowflake is the "little healer." Her compassion and concern for my health keep me jogging at age 76! Her Asian features are topped with a white fur cape (*fake* fur, she stresses). She wears a white snow jacket and black knee-high boots over white pants. When I have a rare headache or pang of arthritis, I think of her and it disappears immediately. Like all Spirits in their world, Snowflake loves animals and receives them into their new home with loving arms and a warm lap. She is St. Francis' favorite angel, and the two of them see that every child in Spirit has a loving pet. More about St. Francis and the garden later!

Rosebud, my little romantic, is the matchmaker who has busybodied tirelessly to bring two loving friends, Richard and me, together from different worlds. She has pale blonde hair worn upswept, sparkling green eyes, and is crowned with a tiara of tiny pink roses. Her pink robe reminds me of the gowns worn by ancient Greek ladies, tied with pink ribbons. She wears little pink sandals laced up over her ankles.

My angels work tirelessly for me, bringing me happiness and safety concerning my health, my relations with my family and others, and in my attitude in all daily occurrences. They have calmed my spirits, kept me close to God, inspired faith and hope in me, given me self-confidence, improved my finances, and brought me the only love of my life, Richard.

II. Others—some on "this side."

Jericho—the "spook." Some time ago, each time I entered my house through the carport door, I heard a strange sound, like a combination whistle and bell. At first I paid little attention, thinking it might be a neighbor's wind chime or something similar. As it continued, always the same, I began to suspect it was not a wind chime at all. It occurred to me that it might be some sort of Spirit. It seemed friendly. One day, as it greeted me, I spoke to it. Evidently this was taken as an invitation to enter the house. I no longer heard the sound outside, but to my irritation I began hearing noises throughout the house—tapping on the walls and lamps, whistles, humming sounds, sighs, and peeps, among others. Jericho, as Richard has dubbed him, and his antics will figure prominently in these excerpts from my communications with Richard and the angels.

I have no image of Jericho. Invisible to me, he is obviously seen by animals, which can't tell me what he looks like—thank heaven! Although at times he is a little pest, he can't be evil or the cats would fear him. I'll have to admit, he is a character and even I have to laugh at him sometimes.

Since they figure in the unfolding of these communications, even though they are not Spirit beings, I must mention my two cats, Mike and Zora.

Mike came to me years ago, while I was working as a secretary at nearby St. Leo University. Each day a big orange-and-white tomcat would visit the campus, entering each department to greet everyone and bum a little handout here and there. I kept a box of treats for him in a bottom desk drawer. At that time he belonged to one of the Abbey brothers, who called him "Speedbump." Someone there evidently didn't want him around, and took him out to the nearby woods and abandoned him there. A few weeks later, he made his way back into the area, and a friend (June, bless her) whom I had alerted found him, frightened and starving, and brought him to me. I was not about to return him to St. Leo, so he became my beloved Mike. He adjusted well with all the loving care and good food, and would give me several years of loyalty and devotion.

Zora lived next door with a young couple. She frequently came into my house through Mike's pet door, availing herself of the furniture and Mike's food. She and Mike were friends, but he wasn't too keen on sharing his territory with her, hissing at her and then ignoring her in the house. Little did I know that one day she would become my own little girl.

As for the author—this is not the story of my life. I hesitated to talk about myself, but Richard says I should be included in the "lineup" so readers know who is writing (rather, co-writing) this. I suppose that makes sense, but I will try to make it as little boring as I can. In knowing me, however, you will understand how great things can happen even to one as unsaintly as I. Sinners, take heart!

I was born under the sign of the Archer in Tampa, Florida. My family: a brilliant father, a beautiful French mother, four bright and handsome brothers and a lovely, super-intelligent sister. I was always—and still am—proud of my family, and hope that somehow I won a little of their pride and affection, though I'm not entirely sure of that. I've always been a sort of maverick, not caring for social status or high achievement. Until recently I never knew I had a learning disability concerning structural and mathematical subjects. I passed algebra by the skin of my teeth and can easily get lost in my own neighborhood—and that's no exaggeration.

Had I been aware of this problem I might have tried harder and, with determination, risen higher in life. I attended the University of Tampa and finished at Florida State University with a B.A. degree. I took summer courses at the University of Havana and the University of Mexico to enhance my majors in Spanish and Inter-American Affairs. I have traveled a lot, and speak several languages, my best being Spanish. I have worked as an airline reservations agent, schoolteacher, in university admissions, as an interpreter and as a social worker. I am an ordained minister of the Universal Church of the Master.

I have been blessed with everything except romantic love. Men considered me independent and I presume this accounts for two failed marriages. I have two beautiful daughters—Noel, an artist and teacher in the Graphic Arts Studio at the University of South Florida, and Rosemary (Rosie) who is married to a successful and very nice Canadian businessman, Roger, in Ontario. Rosie taught Spanish and was an athletic coach before she married. I have no grandchildren.

I accepted my "failure" in love, and thought, now, that's that. Now I have a charming, super-talented, loving and extremely determined Spirit guide who has chosen me as his companion. For a long time, I thought my imagination was running overtime. A relationship with a Spirit? And, I was getting definite message about recording our conversations for a book! Madness. I decided to cease contact. Try dealing with a brick wall! He haunted me unceasingly and wouldn't let up until I gave up and continued to do his bidding, and I loved it. I complained (to deaf ears) that I knew nothing about writing a book. He is in Spirit as he was on Earth, insistent in his pursuits, to put it mildly. As we move along, I will include passages from recorded conversations with Richard and the angels. I hope others will enjoy them as much as I do, and learn as much from them as I did.

Preface

✤

Concerning Richard Tauber

Here's how it all began: One evening several years ago As I watched a PBS program about great singers of the past, Richard Tauber was introduced and sang *Deine Ist Mein Ganzes Herz* (You Are My Heart's Delight) from Franz Lehar's operetta "Land of Smiles." I was intrigued by this charming Austrian tenor with the laughing blue eyes and dark wavy hair. I could not remember him, even though I was always an opera and operetta fan. The following day I did some research at the St. Leo Library and discovered that he was the most highly-acclaimed operetta tenor of all time, and was also very successful in opera, especially Mozart. With my interest in classical music and a large collection of opera records dating from the 1920's, how could I have missed him?

I learned that Richard Tauber was born in Linz, Austria, on May 16, 1891. His father, Richard Anton Tauber, was director of the Chemnitz Stadt Theater. His mother, Elizabeth Denemy, was an operetta soprano. Elizabeth was Roman Catholic, and Richard, the father, was Jewish. Although together and deeply in love, they never married.

Growing up, Richard took naturally to the entertainment world, studying piano and composition. Still very young, he decided to become a singer. His father and several voice teachers tried to discourage him, thinking his voice too small, but he was determined. His father finally relented and arranged for vocal lessons for him.

In 1913, at the age of 22, he made his operatic debut in Chemnitz as Tamino in Mozart's *The Magic Flute*, to rave reviews. This led to a five-year contract with the Dresden Opera in Germany, and to instant fame. He made his home in Vienna and performed in concert and opera all over Europe. He was a member of the Vienna State Opera from 1922 to 1928, and again from 1932 to 1938.

The director and officials there were less than pleased when Richard began performing in operetta, the result of his collaboration with Franz Lehar, who persuaded him to perform in some of his productions. The two men became good friends. "It is his voice I hear when I compose," Lehar said. In 1928, with Richard in the lead, Lehar's operetta "Land of Smiles," the story of an ill-fated romance between the daughter of an Austrian diplomat and a Chinese prince, was a sensation. During his career Richard would sing the best-known song from that operetta, *Deine Ist Mein Ganzes Herz*, in his powerful tenor voice over 10,000 times by his own estimation. Ranging from soft and lyric to powerful and dramatic, or at times funny and rollicking, Richard could handle any part.

Richard's marriage to Carla Vanconti was dissolved and in 1935 he met and married the beautiful British actress Diana Napier, with whom he made several movies. He continued to perform in concert and opera in various parts of the world.

As he was at the peak of his career, Nazi jackboots thundered ominously through the streets of Germany. The *anschluss,* or takeover, of Austria by Adolf Hitler was not to happen until 1938, but Richard could clearly see the sinister writing on the wall. In 1938 he left Germany, never to return. He was later to mourn the loss of many friends and colleagues who had not heeded his warnings, and died in concentration camps such as Auschwitz, Bergen-Belsen and Dachau. He became a British subject in 1940. During World War II he entertained allied forces.

Sadly, by the end of the war he had developed crippling arthritis and cancer of both lungs, but allowed neither condition to curtail his career. In early 1947 he performed in New York in an English production of "Land of Smiles." The audience made him repeat the song "You Are My Heart's Delight" four times, which he sang in that many languages. In London, as he neared the end of his life, the Vienna State

Opera staged a production of Mozart's *Don Giovanni*, and he expressed his desire to sing once more one of his favorite roles, Ottavio. The tenor in that part, Anton Dermota, graciously bowed out for one night, and Richard, though desperately ill, went on in one of the greatest performances of his career. The next day he entered the hospital, and died there on January 8, 1948, at the age of 57. He was interred in Brompton Oratorio, Kensington.

Richard Tauber is remembered as a character, both on and off stage. In public, he made a dashing figure in top hat, opera cloak and his ever-present monocle. Optimistic, tireless, humorous, happy, friendly, lovable and charming, he had a strong, unwavering determination and will which never left him. Nothing ever conquered him—not illness, nor pain, nor Nazi terror, nor bombings (one of which knocked him down a flight of stairs)…not even death. He never gave in to any challenge or threat. He won it all. And he is still winning.

I expected, correctly, that it would be hard to find many of Richard's recordings and movies, as many of them were confiscated by the Third Reich from stores, studios and even private homes, to be burned—symbolically. I have only one of his German movies, the 1933 "Land of Smiles," which possibly had been hidden away by a loyal fan, but suffered defects in sound and picture. Thanks to my nephew Arthur, several of his movies, recordings and documentaries, restored by modern technology, were located via the Internet.

I thought constantly about this fascinating personality, and longed to know him, though I felt this to be beyond reason. He had lived and passed on long ago.

Acknowledgements

Cover artwork provided by Frank Costello of Lexington, MA.

With Thanks to my daughters Noel and Rosie, for their encouragement and support and to my nephew Arthur M. Hale, M. Div., for typing my manuscript, with its chicken scratch handwriting, over (or under) abundance of commas, misspelled words, and misuse of capital and lower case letters, on his computer. God will reward his infinite patience.

I am blessed.

Conversations with My Friends

The Conversations Begin

It was time to communicate with my angels. Through telepathy, they had been answering my prayers for years. I wanted to ask about Richard, and I wanted the contact in writing. I sat down at the table with pen and writing pad, and wrote the date at the top of the page.

What followed comprises the rest of this book.

July 15, 1998.

Sarah: My angels?

Angel: We are here.

S (mentally): I'm imagining this, I'm afraid.

A: Why? You have contacted us many times before. Tell us what you want.

S: How many are you?

A: Five.

S: What are your names?

A: Edelweiss, Rainbow, Snowflake, Dewdrop, and Rosebud.

S: Names related to nature.

A: God created all nature, and all His angels.

S: Who is speaking?

A: Edelweiss, but we are all here.

S: Thank you for your love and guidance.

Edelweiss: As always.

S: I wanted to ask you about someone in Spirit. He "haunts" me, but I am not sure he knows it.

Edelweiss: He knows.

S: Do you know him?

Edelweiss: Richard.

S: Tell me.

Edelweiss: We are in contact with him. When we told him about you, he was surprised and very touched that someone on Earth could be so interested, in a loving way, in him so long after his passing.

S: I love him.

Edelweiss: He knows. The more he learns about your life, character, strong will and your love for him, the greater his feeling for you grows. And you must know that he has been assigned as your Spirit guide.

S: Assigned? By whom?

Edelweiss: The Seraphim.

S: God bless them. And God bless him, and you, my angels. It's hard for me to accept that someone as great on Earth—and in Spirit—could be interested in me. I'm so untalented! What could he possibly see in me?

New Voice: I see a beautiful person.

Edelweiss: That's Richard, butting in! Go ahead, then.

Richard: Thank you, ladies. Sarah, your love of music and the arts is your great talent. You know more about them than many performers on Earth.

S: I wish I had seen you perform in person.

Richard: You will, some day.

S: I don't understand.

Richard: Some day, you will be here with me.

S: How do you know I will?

Richard: I am determined you will.

S: You must be in a very beautiful place. I don't think I am good enough.

Richard: You are a good person. Even though once in a while, do I hear some choice words?

S: You mean cussing? *Moi?*

Richard. *Vous.* It's got to go. I will help you.

S: Good luck!

Edelweiss: Now *we* are butting in! Sarah, this is Richard's first Earth contact since he left there.

S: He sounds like an old pro to me. But I don't want to wear you out with my questions. I've got a zillion of them. Can we talk again soon?

Edelweiss: Very soon.

S: Goodnight, and thank you, my angels. I am very happy.

Edelweiss: Goodnight, Sarah.

The following morning I read the "script" of the previous evening with Richard and my angels. In bright daylight, I was very skeptical. I said to myself that this was all my imagination, and forget it! However, I didn't account for Richard's determination. After a few days of Spirit blitzing, with a sigh of resignation, I sat down to write.

◆   ◆   ◆

July 22, 1998: The Garden of Song .

Sarah: My angels?

Edelweiss: Good evening.

S: I almost decided not to continue our written contacts, thinking I might be imagining it all. When I am with you like this, however, I feel comfortable and experience a sense of reality.

Edelweiss: Richard is happy. He means to have you with him in Spirit one day.

S: He is also bossy.

Edelweiss: You are not accustomed to being monitored. He is your guide and wants the best for you.

S: Is Richard here now?

Edelweiss: Do cows moo?

S: You're funny. Richard?

Richard: Hello, love.

S: Richard, where are you? What is it like and who is there? What do you do there?

Richard: The zillion questions you threatened me with!

S: I want to know all about you and your life there.

Richard: I live through the Light, in a community. The Spirit world, not unlike Earth, is composed of different communities where those of mutual interests and character live together.

S: What is the name of yours?

Richard: We call it the Garden of Song.

S: Do you always remain in one place, or do you interact with or visit other places?

Richard: We visit and are visited by friends and family we knew on the Earth plane.

S: Is it beautiful there?

Richard: More than you could ever imagine until you see for yourself. Our halls and dwellings are of different colors of marble, and though simple are as exquisite as the glories of ancient Greece. They are surrounded by lush gardens with many kinds of bright flowers and plants, sparkling streams, springs, lakes and fountains. The clean, pure air is cool and refreshing.

S: Do you sleep in buildings? In beds?

Richard: We have our own quarters, but we can sleep anywhere, and when we sleep we are invisible.

S: And music? Foolish question!

Richard: you have heard great music on earth: here it is even more beautiful!

S: You said you would sing for me.

Richard: I will. Music is our life. There are no instruments. The music is from Spirit, and our voices combine in joyful harmony.

S: But I can't sing! I will get kicked out.

Richard: You will not get kicked out. Here with me, you will sing. I will teach you.

S: Richard, there is something very serious I want to ask you.

Richard: I hope I can answer your question.

S: Do you still have your cute tummy-tum?

Richard: I look as I did at age 33 on Earth.

S: 33?

Richard: No one in Spirit is over 33, the age of Jesus when He died on the Cross.

S: You had your tummy-tum then?

Richard: I was always chubby. The ladies liked me that way. Some American women told me I looked like a teddy bear. I loved it.

S: I think you're cute.

Richard: *Ja?*

S: And charming and super-talented.

Richard: I like this lady.

S: I'm an old lady now. What do you see in me?

Richard: I've been shown how you were at age 33, with your little girls, playing with your pets. Here you will look the same. But even now you are lovely.

S: Are there pets in Spirit?

Richard: Of all kinds!

S: Will I get to see those pets that have left me? I miss them all.

Richard: All of them.

S: Where do they live?

Richard: In a beautiful garden. We are also allowed to have pets individually here, as on Earth. All in spirit are healthy and happy, lovingly tended.

S: Does St. Francis take care of those in the garden?

Richard: Yes, he receives them when they leave Earth.

S: God bless him. What does he call his garden?

Richard: The Garden of Love. Sarah, I believe you made a large painting of St. Francis in the garden, with some of the animals.

S: Yes, I painted him holding a puppy that had belonged to Rosie, in his arms. Her name was "Sonnet." She died at just a few months.

She was a Brittany Spaniel. They are very courageous. She wagged her little tail with her last breath.

Richard: She is with St. Francis.

S: God bless him, and all his "wards," both big and small. Richard, did you have a pet on Earth?

Richard, Once I brought home a cat, but since my parents traveled so much, and I with them, I had to find her a home. You have had pets all your life.

S: Yes, and especially for my little girls. At one time we had a dog, several cats, fish, turtles, birds, rabbits and mice—a real menagerie! Noel and Rosie knew before they could walk how to handle animals, gently and lovingly. I only had one pedigreed pet in my life. Noel brought home a reddish-blond cocker spaniel from Italy. "Maisie" didn't understand a word of English, having heard only Italian and Spanish. She learned quickly. A tri-lingual dog, if you please! A real character. She is still a handful, I know. Sweet, but very active!

Richard: St. Francis can handle her.

◆   ◆   ◆

September, 1998: About Jericho.

With the passing of summer otherwise peacefully, I began hearing taps and strange noises all over my house. The sounds got worse and frightened me. I contacted my Spirit family and complained.

Edelweiss: Oh-oh! Talk to Richard.

S: Richard, I swear I must have a spook in my house. He raps on the walls and makes obnoxious noises. My cat sees him. Mike's eyes move about watching something I can't see.

Richard: Yes, I know about him. He won't harm you or your cat.

S: How did he get in?

Richard: He says you let him in.

S: He's a big liar! What does he want here?

Richard: He was a lonely, wandering spirit. He found a place with a young heart and a cat. He and Mike are friends.

S: Why here? There are young hearts and cats all over the neighborhood. Who is he?

Richard: I call him Jericho.

S: I'll call him Pestiferous! Last night I was awakened by what sounded like barking. I turned on the light and only Mike was on the bed with me. I will not have spooks barking at my cat!

Richard: I can only say that he is harmless, and loves you and Mike.

S: I hate him. Please make him go away.

Richard: I can't do that, but I can reprimand him when he bothers you.

S: What is your relationship with him?

Richard: I have befriended him for your protection. He trusts and respects me.

S: Protect me yourself—from him. Please get rid of him. I'm losing sleep.

Richard: I will curb some of his exuberance. I promise.

S: I will say goodnight and try to sleep. Do you have anything to say to me?

Richard: I love you. Do you believe me?

S: I don't know. But I love you just the same.

For a few days things were quiet. I hoped Pestiferous had gone. One night, my hopes were shattered by loud knocks on the wall over my bed, followed by a big "whoosh" over my head and a short puff, like someone blowing out a candle, on my cheek. I declared war. The next day, I visited the priest at St. Anthony Catholic Church in San Antonio.

"Father, I've got a spook in my house!"

Father Hughes, keeping a straight face, gave me some anti-spook prayers to recite throughout the house, and a bottle of holy water to enhance the ritual, which I performed that evening. The next day I contacted my angels.

S: If no one sent that spook here, how did Richard find out about him?

Edelweiss: Richard found out from Dewdrop and Rosebud. Jericho won't harm you. He just wants your attention. He protects you.

S: Just how?

Edelweiss: If anyone tries to break into your house or harm you, he will get an unpleasant surprise. And you haven't fallen or hurt yourself since he came to live with you.

S: I'm not accident prone; only once I fell hanging curtains.

Edelweiss: It will not happen again. Richard is here.

S: Richard, I want to tell you about my visit to our local priest regarding our mutual friend, Pestiferous. Father gave me some prayers and holy water. I performed an anti-spook ritual around the house, orating dramatically and flinging holy water all over the place like an idiot.

Richard: How did Jericho react?

S: He loved it! I could sense the little bandit at my side, happily accompanying me every moment of the so-called exorcism. I wish he had a butt. I'd kick it.

Richard: Luckily for him, he doesn't have one.

S: Richard, I want him out, *now.* How would you like having a spook in your house?

Richard: I can't remove him.

S: You must control him. I will go to a *botanica* (religious/witchcraft store) and get black candles and other voodoo supplies to exorcise him.

Richard: Don't do that! It will harm only you. Let me deal with him. We need a devious way to subdue him. I have an idea.

◆   ◆   ◆

November 1988. Richard and Sarah.

S: My angels?

Edelweiss: Where have you been the past few weeks?

S: The holidays are approaching. Busy—busy—busy! Is Richard here to talk with me?

Edelweiss: Do cows moo?

Richard: Is the Rabbi Jewish?

S: Richard! I love you and your cute tummy-tum.

Richard: You only love me for my tummy-tum.

S: You're all cute! I want to ask you, are there other couples, like husband and wife, in spirit? Why isn't the lady you were married to with you?

Richard: Don't be nosy. There are things not necessary for you to know. Not yet.

S: You always want to know about *me*!

Richard: I know all about you.

S: Good or bad?

Richard: Good, except when you cuss. Tsk, tsk.

S: I cuss at Pestiferous. By the way, he has been very quiet. How did you do it?

Richard: I threatened him with the guillotine.

S: Does he know what it is?

Richard, No, but he doesn't like the sound of it. I now have a weapon!

S: A "Coup for the Boo," eh?

Richard: That's a good slogan.

S: Richard, I know about you only from articles written by others. Talk to me about your life on Earth. I know you were happy here. Do you miss it very much?

Richard: To Sarah…the Earth I loved.

As I have told you, the world I now live in is beautiful, and I am very happy and blessed in my spirit home. Still, I remember my life on Earth with great nostalgia. You, Sarah, after so long, have brought me contact with the Earth I loved. I was, as one might say, "born in a trunk" in Linz, where my father at the time was conducting. From birth I learned to love music and all the arts. Music was magic, to me one of the great gifts of God. How could anyone be anything but happy around beautiful sounds? No bad vibrations could penetrate my happiness. It never occurred to me that I could fail at anything. Ego? I won't deny it! But it was more than that. We absorb into our lives only what our spirit allows. How could we lose? Also, think of the beauties of nature! Just to see and smell a rose brings one closer to God. The soothing patter of raindrops is God's promise of growth and fresh air. No one who has ever seen a sunrise over the mountains or a sunset over the ocean can doubt God. To me, God has two names: Father God, and Mother Nature, symbolizing the love and artistic completion of mankind—man and woman.

I remember one sunny afternoon when I was about five, going with my father for a walk on a mountain incline near Salzburg, where my parents were performing. When we reached a plateau, hand in hand we stopped to look at all the beauty around us. In the pure Alpine air, the world was all beautiful colors: the gold of the sun over the green mountainside lavishly spread with bright flowers under a cloudless blue sky. In the distance, we saw a falcon gracefully circling for small prey. I was entranced. I looked up at my father, and asked, "Father, is this Heaven?" He laughed and answered, "Very close." I was delighted to know that in another life I would dwell in such a wonderland. Thank God for all His blessings on Earth and in Spirit. And for you, Sarah. Now tell me of your thoughts, your joys and sadness. And your dreams.

Sarah: To Richard…the Earth I know.

I have a mental picture of you on the mountain holding your father's hand, gazing in awe at the wonders you experienced closely for the first time. What a darling you must have been!

My life in Florida was very different. I was surrounded by water, and by the lakes, rivers and beaches where we went each summer.

When I was 15, we moved from Tampa to a lovely country home in an area now known as Land O' Lakes. I rode a school bus every morning to a Catholic academy, Holy Name, about 20 miles east in the small town of San Antonio where I now live. World War II was blazing, and all my brothers and my sister were represented by five blue stars displayed in the window of our home. Thank God, none was replaced with a gold one! In my senior year, a friend of mine, Rosemary, entered the academy and wanted someone to walk to school with each day through the woods from her house, which was the old clubhouse of a defunct golf course. I was delighted to stay with the family during the week. They treated me as one of them!

I have lived in several different countries, each for a short while. It was a better education than all my years in college. People, even with different customs, languages and religions, always react happily to just two things—love and respect. Other things are unimportant in forming friendships.

After college, I married—twice! And yet, I don't think I ever loved anyone. Until now. In the past I have felt resentment and bitterness towards certain people. For what?! It's past tense, all of it. That's why I needed you, Richard. To follow your example. There was more by far of pain, anxiety, and sadness in your life and yet you never let it get to you. My problems were and are so small. Thank you for your love and guidance, and your shining example. You were great on Earth and you are even greater in Spirit. I am blessed to have you and my beautiful angels.

◆　　　◆　　　◆

December 15, 1998

S: My angels! Roll call!

Edelweiss: All here: Edelweiss, Rainbow, Dewdrop, Snowflake and Rosebud.

S: Do you like my Christmas tree?

Edelweiss: The little angel at the top of the tree is the same one you always put at the top of the tree when your daughters were growing up.

S: Yes, Noel and Rosie always had a "trim the tree" party with their little crowd for buffet and decorating the tree. The decorations are worn now, but I always use the same ones (that have survived) for sentimental reasons. One year, the only one in the crowd old enough to drive was a 16-year-old Jewish boy named Bruce. The others dressed him like a Christmas tree and sent him out for more ice. As he was leaving the convenience store with the ice he turned around in the doorway and said to the bewildered clerks, "What's the matter? Haven't you ever seen a Hanukkah bush before?"

Rosebud: I like the little kissing angels under the tree. Everyone is in love at Christmas time!

Rainbow: And so many beautiful colors! The winking lights remind me of the stars on our beautiful clear nights.

S: Unfortunately, we don't see much of the stars as we did on Earth at one time, because of smog conditions. On a windjammer cruise in the Caribbean with Rosie for her college graduation in 1975, I lay on the upper deck one night and marveled at the brilliance of the stars, and recalled seeing them just so as a young person. My mother pointed out the Milky Way, trailing across the sky like a shimmering bridal veil!

Snowflake: You had a spiritual feeling, remote from Earth's problems, with God as you beheld His wonders.

Rosebud: With no pollution! And, speaking of wonders, guess who is here?

S: Not Richard?

All Angels: Do cows moo?

Richard: You enjoy preparing for Christmas?

S: My favorite time of the year. Tell me about Christmas in Spirit. Do you celebrate as we do on our religious holidays?

Richard: The only holidays we coordinate with Earth festivities are the Nativity and the Resurrection, for universal homage to our Holy Baby and Savior.

S: Tell me about Christmas.

Richard: Our celebration is a festival of song and lights. Our great choir forms three tiers high in the heavens.

S: How many are you?

Richard: Who counts?

S: What do you sing?

Richard: We compose our carols of joy and thanks for our Holy Baby, and sometimes we nostalgically sing some of those carols such as *Silent Night* and *Oh, Holy Night*. We remember our happy days on Earth with our families and friends as we sing them.

S: What are the songs you compose?

Richard: You will hear them here.

S: The lights?

Richard: Our candles, for one. What is Christmas without candles?

S: Don't they melt?

Richard: In Spirit, nothing melts.

S: How do you light them? With matches?

Richard: They light because we want them to. There is no lighting, no burning, just a golden glow.

S: Do you see the star of Bethlehem?

Richard: It glows exactly as it did almost 2000 years ago as it led the three wise men to the newborn King. Every star in the heavens glows brighter at this time than at any other time. It is a beautiful spectacle. We are all very emotional, feeling the same joy as did the three kings as they bowed before the tiny Holy One.

S: Do you have a Christmas tree?

Richard: We have a wonderful tree each year that grows in our garden, with no need to cut any down. It bears many colored lights, each one a special prayer for a loved one on Earth, and many for the special intentions of Jesus, beginning with Love.

S: And Faith, Hope, and Charity?

Richard: If there were more love on Earth, those and all other virtues would abound in course, as unselfish love is the basis of all goodness and happiness.

S: God bless all of you in your lovely Spirit home, for your love, prayers and guidance for us on Earth who are dependent on all blessings.

January 1999

I watched the Times Square exuberance ring in the New Year. Dear Lord, I thought, this is the last year of the millennium! I Thought about the past years of my life and all the technological advances accomplished: miracle drugs, surgery, cellular phones, television, computers, astronauts walking on the moon, to name only a few. Somehow, these things don't surprise me. Mankind (and that includes womankind!) in spite of all our foibles and follies and problems, is a success. We've done it, we're doing it, and will continue to do it—succeed! Thank God for all His blessings.

◆   ◆   ◆

February 1999: Morris.

My euphoria brought on by the beautiful holiday season was about to be shattered. Every January my brother Morris and his wife Anna Bess always came to Florida to spend the winter months away from the snows and winds of Illinois, to sun and fish on the east coast beaches. Noel and I were scheduled to visit them in Melbourne in the latter part of February. Early in the month I was awakened at dawn by the telephone. It was Anna Bess. Morris had suffered a heart attack and was hospitalized. I was there in two hours. When I arrived, he seemed to be recovering somewhat. The next day, he fumed about being restrained, and checked himself out of the hospital.

He was at peace back at the beach cottage, walking around the yard and gazing from the gazebo over his beloved Atlantic Ocean.

On February 18 he passed away. On March 18 his ashes were interred in Arlington National Cemetery. I was there. My favorite brother, who always made me feel special and loved, was gone. On a special place atop an antique bookcase in my living room I have a memorial plaque issued by the University of Illinois commemorating his unique and productive life, pictures of him showing off a big catch, of his wife, daughters and me at Arlington (Anna Bess holding the folded flag), and one of him and Anna Bess relaxing in front of a fireplace. There is a votive candle and an angel next to the plaque. A small vase of flowers is always by his picture. My Spirit gossips tell me he is very amused by his "shrine"—he never took himself seriously. He says I should paint the ceiling over the shrine like the Sistine Chapel, hire the Mormon Tabernacle Choir, and set off fireworks to celebrate! Just like him. He always had to joke about everything. He hasn't changed.

◆   ◆   ◆

March 18, 1999: Midnight.

S: My angels?

Edelweiss: Isn't this a little late for you, especially after such a long, emotional day and plane trip? You must be tired. You have to work tomorrow.

S: No, I've been running on adrenaline all day. Just glad I could attend Morris' impressive services at the National Cemetery. I was so proud that my brother was being so honored for his remarkable legal career as a colonel in the Air Force.

Snowflake: We've been with you.

S: I felt your presence, especially on the plane returning to Tampa International Airport. The air got very turbulent, and I prayed for by angels to quiet things down. It stopped immediately. Thank you, angels. Rosebud, do I hear mooing?

Rosebud: Richard is here, shifting impatiently.

Richard: Did you enjoy your ride on the maintenance cart?

S: You don't miss anything, do you? Yes, at the airport I couldn't find my car in the long-term parking lot, and a kind maintenance worker driving a cart offered me a ride. I jumped on the back. It was very uncomfortable, but I was most grateful to find my car. When I got home, Mike was waiting for me in the driveway.

Richard: At Arlington, did you see the gravesites of any of your great statesmen or military heroes?

S: I saw only Morris'. Some day, I hope to return to see Morris' again, and other gravesites of America heroes.

Richard: Your brother's service must have been impressive.

S: Very military, symbolic, and touching, especially when "Taps" was played. Afterwards, all the family present including nieces and nephews, great-niece and nephews, and one great-great niece, one month old, met in the main building lobby. One of my great nieces, Krista, whom I had not seen for a while, drew my attention immediately because of her remarkable resemblance to my grandmother, whose picture I have on my wall. A real fifth-generation carbon copy! I will pack up the portrait and send it right away to Krista.

This grandmother of mine, Marie Elodie Allain, would be interesting to anyone involved in the metaphysical. She was born in 1841 of French parents on a cotton plantation in Iberville Parish, Louisiana, near the Mississippi River. I have never believed in or condoned slavery, but many interesting stories have been passed down about Elodie and her relationship to the many workers on the Allain plantation. The one she loved the most was the daughter of an African chieftan, who told Elodie about her capture by slave traders. She was at a spring one day, about to drink, and as she bent over the water, she saw the reflection of two men leaning over to grab her. Royalty became enslaved.

As are most people of African descent, the slaves were very spiritual, and were impressed with Elodie's natural psychic and spiritual gifts. She could communicate at a very early age with spirits, and astounded her family and friends with her automatic writing, receiving messages in the very handwriting of those sending form Spirit. The local priest heard about it, and paid a visit to the plantation. He denounced her writing as "the work of the Devil," and forbade her further contacts with the dead. As a good Catholic girl, she obeyed.

The story of the African princess, whose assigned Christian name I can't remember, stayed in my mind. I don't know if the dream I had one night when I was a child was the power of suggestion spurring my imagination or indeed a real visitation from the beautiful princess. I saw her standing tall and strong in a brightly colored wrap-around dress and bead jewelry, gazing at me pleasantly. I spoke to her. "Who are you?" "She said, "My name is Dakara. I loved Elodie." The she smiled and was gone.

The beautiful lady has never returned to me. One day, I will see her again. At the end of the Civil War, all the slaves were freed. Some stayed on the plantation; others went forth to a new life with the good wishes of the Allain family.

During the war, the house was quartered by federal troops. I was curious about the behavior of the men towards the family and property. My mother told me, "Mama said they were just a lot of nice boys a long way from home."

Richard, If you're still here, I didn't mean to ramble on so.

Richard: I'm here, and I loved your story. I think that priest was wrong in suppressing your grandmother's spiritual gifts. We in Spirit are just as sad to leave our loved ones on Earth as you are to lose us. We are so happy when you call us. Our communications, though some would think them strange or impossible, are very normal.

S: Richard, what is Morris doing now?

Richard: He is resting, for a short while. Then he will begin his indoctrination. He will miss his family, but will have a happy existence in Spirit. Anna Bess will feel his presence, as he will guide her. They are very close, and will be together again one day.

S: Yes, they were. I love them both dearly.

Richard: More traumatic than death is birth on the Earth plane, though each is an abrupt transition. A newborn infant is traumatized not only from a smart whack on his little behind, but from being in an entirely different physical situation, having to breathe on his own, facing the glaring lights of the delivery room and hearing the conversations of the medical personnel, instead of being in the quiet darkness of his mother's womb.

Leaving the Earth plane is a bewildering experience. I remember the impression of being wheeled down the hospital corridor on one of those gurneys that roll smoothly and quietly, and thinking, now where are they taking me? Then slowly I came to the realization that I was no longer on Earth. I was floating in space, through what seemed like a tunnel with sides of fluctuating white clouds. I didn't know where I was going, but I was not afraid, only sad to be leaving my beloved Earth. I began to cry. Then I saw a light ahead of me, that got brighter and brighter as I approached the end of the tunnel, but it did not hurt my eyes. I felt comforted, and curious! I couldn't wait to enter that light! As it enveloped me I fell peacefully asleep.

S: And when you awakened?

Richard: I was in a beautiful garden under a pink marble shed, lying on a soft bed with fragrant, bright flowers of all kinds surrounding me. I was a bit disoriented at first. There were two men and two women at my side.

S: What were they like?

Richard: Not strange at all, but dressed differently and comfortably, the men in pants and shirts with round necks and long sleeves, the women in gowns very much like the muumuus of your island people.

S: Were they dressed all in white? Were they angels? Did they have wings? Harps?

Richard: You've been seeing too many spirit movies. Their clothes were in different light, what I call "rainbow" colors. I asked them, "Am I in a hospital?" One of the men laughed and said, "No, Richard, you are no longer on Earth. There's no need to be afraid. How do you feel?" I said, "I feel no pain." He said, "You will never feel pain again. Welcome to our garden." And that was my introduction to Spirit.

S: Did it take long to adjust to your new life and surroundings?

Richard: They knew just how to make me feel welcome! I was soon taken to sing with a wonderful choir. To sing again! My heart sang with my voice. I was at home.

S: What a beautiful story. Will I really be there with you?

Richard: If you quit swearing.

S: Oh, Richard! It's mainly at Pestiferous. And in traffic sometimes. I don't realize I've cussed until after somebody almost rams me.

Richard: You won't have that problem here. We need no automobiles or airplanes; we get around on our own very well. With your Pestiferous we will deal according to his current travesty. He hates being in the doghouse.

S: How does he get around to both worlds?

Richard: He is a spirit. He can be there in a second and back in another.

S: I'll never understand spirits.

Richard: You will, when you're one.

◆   ◆   ◆

April 4, 1999: Easter.

S: Happy Easter!

Edelweiss: And to you, Sarah. May all the blessings of this holy day be yours.

S: I thought of you during services, and wished I could be two people so one of me could be with you.

Edelweiss: Richard has a lot to tell you.

Richard: Thank you, ladies.

S: Tell me about your celebration.

Richard: As you know, Jesus visits us here in the garden at Easter-tide.

S: Please tell me all about Him. What does He look like? What did He say and do?

Richard: Jesus is not like most illustrations of Him, with golden-brown hair and blue eyes, though just as beautiful! He was born among the Mediterranean people, and has dark hair and eyes and olive skin, created to be like His neighbors and not stand out like a sore thumb, to use an American expression. He has, of course, a very kindly expression, with a twinkle in His eye. A soft golden glow surrounds His entire body. He has a great sense of humor and loves to laugh. Very strong, He moves about energetically. He always wants to know about everyone in the garden, with a charming way of putting all at ease, talking about families and friends on Earth and joking with everyone. You on Earth think He is wonderful? A million times greater than that! He is man, Spirit, Savior, comedian, tragedian, athlete, lover of man and all nature. He is the Son of God. He is God. The greatest friend man or animal ever had. Even all of this cannot describe His magnificence. How blessed we are!

S: Will I really ever get to talk to Him?

Richard: If you behave!

S: Richard, you *didn't* tell Him I cuss. I'll kill you.

Richard: I told Him an old boyfriend of yours called you "Garbage Mouth."

S: I'm dead. What did He say?

Richard: He roared with laughter. He said He expects me to deal with you effectively. Remember that.

S: Bossy Britches!

Richard: Everything I do is directed toward having you here with me some day.

S: I know. Truthfully, it means everything to me.

Rosebud: Jesus likes to make us laugh. He says Dewdrop and I gossip, and wanted to hear all the "latest."

Snowflake: I wonder where He got that idea.

Dewdrop: He knows we have to pry sometimes to be able to deal with problems that may arise on Earth.

S: You are all darlings. I don't know what I'd do without you.

Edelweiss: Jesus told us to take care of you

S: Blessed is His Name! Tell me about your Easter with Jesus.

Rosebud: It was lovely. Jesus wants everything simple. We all gathered among the beautiful plants and trees at the big fountain.

S: What is it like?

Rainbow: It is round and of the finest pink marble. It spouts in the center like a—what do you call it?

S: An artesian well?

Snowflake: Yes. We call it the Fountain of Life. We love to sit around on its circular rim and listen to the sound of Life splashing cleanly and happily about us.

S: Are there fish in the fountain?

Snowflake: No, they swim freely in larger areas, the rivers and lakes.

S: Tell me about your sessions with Jesus.

Rainbow: We talked about our Spirit vocations. He is interested in and supportive of all we do, patiently answering our questions and offering very constructive advice.

S: Richard, He must love to hear you sing.

Richard: We sing joyfully for Him. He calls us His artists.

S: Tell me about Mary, His mother.

Richard: She is beloved and honored by all. She is the Mother of God and the greatest lady who ever lived or will ever live. She is here when we need her, to comfort us when there is a tragedy on Earth that brings us sorrow, such as a burdened friend or a relative who needs our prayers and support and we are no longer there to give comfort. She holds our hands, and we all pray together for God's blessing. She is so gentle and yet so powerful, a sublime example of the strength in meekness and kindness. The greatest men and women on Earth are those who are gentle of spirit.

S: I love to talk to you and listen.

Richard: You don't always listen! A while ago I heard a word that would cause a longshoreman with lumbago to blush.

S: Don't pick on longshoremen. They'll sue you. Besides, it wasn't that bad. I cuss now only at your friend Pestiferous. I can't exactly wear a halo around him. By the way, do you have a halo?

Richard: Don't go around telling people Richard Tauber has a halo. They will laugh. You know everyone has an aura. These auras or emanations of light around our bodies on Earth can be seen under a special light.

S: Ultra-violet.

Richard: Some of your metaphysicians can see these auras, but generally they are seen only in the laboratory. The Holy Ones, Jesus, Mary, the saints and angels, manifest bright but soft auras. Great artists from the early times spiritually visualized these auras and painted them above their heads as a circle of light. The Mexican patron saint, La Virgen de Guadalupe, whose image appeared on the cloak of a peon, Juan Diego, is shown with a bright golden aura surrounding her entire body. This is the most accurate depiction of her aura, since the image was given by the lady herself.

S: Everyone's aura is different.

Richard: Yes, and it changes according to mood and state of health.

S: Mine?

Richard: A beautiful shade of green like jadeite, unless you are fuming at Jericho.

S: And longing to choke him. Yours is gold, isn't it?

Richard: It fluctuates with blues, greens and gold. The latter, when I sing! Gold is the color of fulfillment. I feel complete when I sing. Work on that beautiful green aura, Sarah. Green is for growth. One must grow spiritually every day of his life on Earth and in Spirit.

S: I love green! Tell me about the angels' auras.

Richard: Edelweiss' is white. It fluctuates around her head and shoulders and swirls to her ankles. Rainbow's is varied, as her namesake phenomenon she loves so well. Snowflake's is blue with many tiny silver sparkles. Rosebud's is a soft romantic (of course) pink. Dewdrop's is a soft blue.

S: Now I have a complete picture of them. Maybe some day they will be "immortalized" by an artist. Richard, can you explain the Holy Trinity?

Richard: How can you expect me to explain what even His Holiness the Pope cannot explain? The Father, Invisible Lord and Power of the universe, created His Son in human form to walk among the good and the sinners, to prove to them His love by dying for them on the Cross. The Holy Spirit is the Power and enlightenment emanating from the Hand of God that inspires and strengthens us. Don't ask me how He did it. No one but God knows that.

S: Does the Holy Spirit have a form?

Richard: No one has ever seen Him. On Earth He is depicted as a dove, powerful in His flight for peace and love. I felt his power once on Earth, as I lay very ill, facing the end of my life. I was sad and frightened. I prayed for God's forgiveness and a happy afterlife, then I fell into a fitful sleep. In the middle of the night I awakened with a feeling I can hardly describe, of relief, of happiness, faith, love, and strengthening of mind, body and spirit. It was glorious. I left the Earth in peace.

S: Richard, is there life on other planets?

Richard: I asked Jesus about that. He said that for now, Earth is giving Him enough problems to keep Him occupied! So for now, no definite answer. We are, however, keeping track of reports of UFOs sighted from Earth. Keep an open mind.

S: And, oh, yes! What does Jesus wear?

Richard: The Biblical artists have painted His clothing and sandals accurately as worn in that area during those times.

◆   ◆   ◆

May 16, 1999.

S: Happy birthday, Richard!

Richard: The flowers are lovely. Thank you!

S: You have two birthdays, your Earth birthday today and your Spirit birthday on January 8. You came in the spring and left in the winter. Richard, are birthdays celebrated in your world?

Richard: Each time we welcome a new arrival in the garden, we have a joyful celebration honoring our new member and give thanks to God for our safe journey through the Light into our wonderful new life.

S: Do the new artists adjust to their new surroundings as quickly as you?

Richard: Since we keep everyone busy, it doesn't take them long to feel at home.

S: I have a video that features you, Leo Slezak and Joseph Schmidt.[1] On Earth, Schmidt suffered a tragic end during World War II in Switzerland, where he entered illegally seeking asylum and was thrown into an internment camp. He was diagnosed as a malingerer and died with heart problems and pneumonia unattended at the age of 38. So much for the benevolent and highly praised Swiss neutrality during Herr Hitler's Third Reich! I hope he has found the happiness he was denied on Earth in a beautiful heavenly home.

Richard: He has.

Whatever happened to your home in Vienna that was confiscated by the Nazis after you left?

Richard: Eventually it was returned to me and sold. Meanwhile I had a home and a wife in England and became a British subject.

---

1.   This videotape, *Tenors of the 78 Era, Volume II*, and many others can be obtained from the Bel Canto Society, **www.belcantosociety.org/**

S: Thank God you were safe. Terrible things happened, that I hope are never forgotten. I read or see on TV about groups of "neo-Nazis" not only in Germany, but all around the world, even in America. I dread it.

Richard: It will never be as before. There are too many against them. These thugs can cause some trouble, but will never win. In Spirit it is one of our main concerns, and we pray constantly. There will always be troublemakers, terrorists and fanatics who can inflame others with their foulness, but will ultimately lose. They are rotten cowards who gain power by bullying and backstabbing, two signs of the utmost cowardice. The world has had enough!

S: Please never stop praying for this cause.

Richard: Never.

July 4, 1999.

Edelweiss: Happy fourth! Sounds like everyone is having a good time. We are happy for you in your celebration of liberty.

S: Mike is hiding under the couch away from the fireworks in the neighborhood. I will stay in and watch the spectacles on TV tonight. And no storms around now!

Rainbow: Ta-da!

Edelweiss: You're getting a little breather this month, but fasten your seat belts when August comes.

S: Will we be hit here?

Edelweiss: Pray—keep in touch—we will strengthen each other.

S: Do I strengthen you?

Edelweiss: The line of communication between us is a strong bond. One end won't work without the other. It's team work.

S: Then we are a team!

Edelweiss: Better believe it!

S: Bless all of you! Rainbow, keep those colors flying! Dewdrop, protect our little home. Snowflake, help me keep strong. Rosebud, keep Richard in line. Edelweiss, keep all of them in line.

Edelweiss: And Richard will keep *you* in line!

S: I rather like the idea. Is Richard here for me?

All angels: Do cows moo?

Richard: I hope I can keep you in line. Remember what Jesus said.

S: Please don't give up. I want to be with you! Richard, I have a problem with Mike. Can we do something about his habit of bringing in critters? Day and night I am chasing leaping frogs, scurrying lizards, birds flapping all over the house, fat little field mice waddling about, crickets, and even a mole that bit me as I tried to rescue it, the ingrate. I had to get a tetanus shot at the Health Department.

Richard: He is bringing you gifts. You can see that he doesn't hurt them. All you can do is chase the critters, as you call them, and turn them loose outside.

S: A cardinal clamped onto my hand when I caught him last week. He fainted when I dislodged him, and I had to revive him before he was able to fly to his mate, who hovered anxiously nearby. The things I have to do for the preservation of the country's fauna! And, problem number two. It happened last night.

Richard: Jericho?

S: Oil your guillotine. Around midnight, I was awakened by what sounded like "glubba glubba rubble bubble gargle blubba."

Richard: He's trying to talk.

S: Could he learn?

Richard: I hope he doesn't cuss if he does. He just wants your attention.

S: Are you sure he doesn't have a butt?

Richard: No. Let me handle this.

◆   ◆   ◆

July 8, 1999.

Richard: How's Mike?

S: He had his teeth cleaned today. He did real well and was bright and alert when I picked him up. As soon as he got in the house, he jumped up on the couch and started pawing at Jericho, who, even though I can't see him, I know was paying his respects to Mike upon his return from the vet.

Snowflake: He doesn't like for Mike to leave the house. When you put Mike in the car he's nervous, afraid Mike might not return.

S: He's been awfully good lately. Richard must have really blessed him out.

Snowflake: He respects Richard and doesn't want him to be angry with him.

S: Thank God for His blessings! And for Richard's guillotine.

Rosebud: Here's Richard.

S: Richard, what did you do to Pestiferous? He's been awfully good—*too* good.

Richard: He's in the doghouse. Let it go at that. Actually, I rather enjoy the little rascal.

S: Good. Come and get him.

Richard: It's not that simple. Trust me. All will be well. He won't leave you or Mike.

S: Thank you for dealing with him. I swear I wouldn't know what to do.

Richard: What you always do. Cuss him out.

S: That doesn't faze him. Why is he so insensitive?

Richard: He isn't. He loves you.

S: Great. That's all I need. Can others be so fortunate?

Richard: You'd be surprised. There are many good spirits who can help a lot. Your niece Linda told you she feels the presence of two friendly spirits in her home, and she loves it.

S: They won't give her any numbers to play, but they are always there if she's a little tired, and she senses them comforting her.

Richard: You see? I'm glad she told you. Even if she doesn't win the lottery, that's okay, she thinks.

S: Well, hers don't whistle or go "glubba glubba" at her when she's trying to sleep. I'm glad, however, he's not a pervert. For that, thank God.

Richard: No, he isn't. He's just a mischievous kid, trying to get your attention.

S: He certainly does that. How would you like to awaken during the night to a coyote howling?

Richard: How do you know he was imitating a coyote?

S: I stayed overnight in a motel on the edge of the desert once. Early in the morning when everyone was sleeping, garbage cans started banging around, followed by a chorus of loud howling. I rang the office. The switchboard operator told me, "Nothing to worry about. It's just the coyotes in from the desert to raid the garbage cans and drink pool water, and then thank us with their harmony." So don't tell me I don't recognize a coyote howling when I hear one.

Richard: Try to be patient.

S: Use your guillotine.

With Pestiferous behaving, the rest of July 1999 passed peacefully, and I indulged in my two favorite activities, sleeping and thrift-shopping at Salvation Army, Goodwill, St Vincent de Paul, etc. Almost all of my wardrobe is "thrifty," and I dress as well as anyone. It's fun. Sometimes I wonder who previously owned these things I wear. I get a "vibe" sometimes. Once I bought a pretty little gray sweater at Goodwill. When I put it on one morning for work, I had a warm, loving feeling. My angels told me a sweet little lady had owned that sweater, and when she passed, her daughter donated her things in hope that her mother's belongings would make someone happy. And yes, they do. I love my sweater; it's my favorite. Bless you, sweet lady, wherever you are.

◆   ◆   ◆

August 1999: Hurricanes!

Edelweiss' hurricane predictions lived up to all the TV weathermen's forecast—all bad. Arlene, in June, had blitzed Louisiana. Bret, on August 11, was heading this way.

S: My angels!

Rainbow: On storm watch, all present.

S: Bret is headed this way. Please divert him—he's a stinker. I'm having a tizzy.

Edelweiss: We're working on it. Richard is also having a tizzy. Will have to calm you both down. Here he is.

S: Richard, how can I stay calm when my guide is having a tizzy?

Richard: I've been anxious, but I know the angels can handle the storms. Hurricanes are not in my résumé! Are you and Mike prepared for emergency?

S: The bathtub is filled with fresh water and the pantry full for both Mike and me. We have candles and matches. The storms can do a lot of damage but thankfully do not last long.

Richard: Will you be safe at home?

S: As safe as anywhere. If the electricity stays on I will play your records and know you are watching out for me.

Richard: I don't want anything to happen to you or Mike, or your property.

S: Mike will courageously crawl under the heavy couch until the thunder, lightning and winds subside. We'll be fine!

Richard: I'll be close by. Goodnight, my one and only love.

Thank God for my angels! By the weekend, Bret had turned northward toward Texas. Imagine the Texans' relief when he went over uninhabited land and died out! On September 19 a bad one in the Gulf was heading this way. "Harvey" was also re-routed in another direction. Others had not been so fortunate. A couple of weeks before, "Gert" had virtually wiped out parts of North Carolina. These poor people lost all of their material things in the floods, and were thanking God for all those who were saved by brave, hardworking crews. Even stranded pets were rescued! I hope I have that much courage if it ever happens here.

Rainbow: We'll weather it together!

◆   ◆   ◆

October 15, 1999.

S: Richard, how do you strangle a spook? You're not going to believe this.

Richard: If it's about Jericho, I will believe it.

S: Last night, I was awakened at some godforsaken hour by a loud whistle, and Mike jumped up on the bed. I decided to ignore it, and just as I was about to drift off, a big battle royal ensued with those two romping all over the bed, with my legs and feet getting the worst of it. I lost my temper, but I won't tell you what I said.

Richard: You don't have to. A dense purple fog was rising from your house high into the atmosphere.

S: It wasn't *that* bad. Please behead him!

Richard: I will oil and sharpen the guillotine. In the meantime, write 1000 times: I shall not cuss. Let me handle him.

S: And moreover, our annual Rattlesnake Festival here in San Antonio was cancelled because there is a storm, which I don't think, will hit here. I was looking forward to the barbecued chicken, arts and crafts, animal petting zoo for the kids (and me!), country music and dessert sales by the Holy Name sisters.

Richard: The festival was named for a snake?

S: When this area was populated in the 19th century, the men would go out each year at this time to rid the area of rattlesnake overpopulation. Then they gave a prize for the biggest catch and had a few beers, and from then it grew each year into a big deal. This hasn't been my week!

Richard: Just think of all your blessings.

S: You are right.

◆   ◆   ◆

October 31, 1999.

S: My angels.

Edelweiss! Trick or Treat! Things should get interesting tonight. All Hallows Eve—or, as you call it, Halloween.

S: Services will be held tomorrow for All Saints' Day, but tonight belongs to the kids, who will dress up in their costumes and go from door to door for treats. What do you think of the custom? Some church leaders denounce it as a sacrilege and feel the children should be involved in religious activities instead, or dress as saints and angels for a private or school function.

Edelweiss: The children mean no harm in their fun, even in some of their more weird and ghoulish outfits, mainly the boys! There's nothing wrong in their having a good time.

S: I'm glad you see no offense in this. The adults enjoy it as much as the kids. One Halloween when my daughters were small, almost all the neighborhood kids were ill with colds, and Noel and Rosie were very disappointed to have no one to march with. Suddenly I asked, "How would you like to go to New Orleans tonight?" (Do cows moo? Do beagles wag their tails?) They were packed before I got off the phone with airline reservations! I missed all the ghosts and goblins, but we had a wonderful weekend in the old French Quarter. I showed the girls

Pirates' Alley, into which my aunt and a little friend of hers had sneaked many years ago looking for a *real* pirate. (They did exist in those days.) As they passed by one door, a big, swarthy man wearing a bandanna around his head and a gold loop earring in his ear glared out at them, and they ran in terror. I'm sure the "pirate" had a good laugh.

The girls enjoyed visiting the gravesite of my Confederate grandfather, William, in the old St. Louis Cemetery. Another of my aunt's stories: sitting on her father's lap after the Civil War, she braided his beard into two pigtails and tied them with pink ribbons. He forgot and took her down the street for ice cream. He must have made quite a picture!

My other grandfather was a Federal soldier in the Civil War. I attended a metaphysical church once, where the minister giving messages asked me if I had two grandfathers in the war, that one was present to greet me.

I asked her, "What color is his uniform?"

She answered, "This is the one in blue."

I said, "God bless him, he is welcome."

Joseph was born in England. After the war he married a Pennsylvania Dutch lady named Sarah, and they moved to Dickson, Tennessee, where my father, Arthur, was born.

I seem to have gone off on a tangent, angels!

Edelweiss: It was interesting! Thank you for sharing some of your thoughts and experiences. Richard is here.

S: Richard, the children will be here is a little while with their spook outfits.

Richard: I'm afraid of ghosts.

S: You're funny. When you were a child, were there any costume parties for kids similar to ours?

Richard: Only to special private costume affairs. We were allowed to dress as animals, clowns, and storybook characters. We even got prizes. I once won a first prize as Pinocchio. Since my parents were performers and make-up artists, some of the parents felt it was unfair.

S: Jealousy! It happens everywhere. Did you have a long wooden nose?

Richard: Yes, and I kept bumping into things. The children pulled my nose, but only in fun!

S: Now I will put out the candy in preparation for the goblins.

Richard: Good night, love—have fun with your little visitors.

S: Good night! I will.

◆　　　◆　　　◆

Thanksgiving 1999.

Edelweiss: Did you have a good day?

S: You know I did! We all gathered at a friend's house in the country. He has beautiful horses.

Snowflake: It's a good thing we have animals in Spirit, or you would refuse to live here.

S: So would you! Snow, are there working animals there, like oxen, camels, etc.?

Snowflake: No, all animals are for pets only. There are no problems for animals. *We* work!

S: And that work?

Edelweiss: Our principal duties are guidance and prayers for those still on Earth. We like to work in our lovely gardens. The plants, like the animals, thrive on our loving care. We have our magnificent choir. We help the new arrivals to adjust and grow. Our festivals Richard mentioned have to be organized. It's a good thing we don't have to live by the clock here! We'd never get done! Our work is a blessing from God. You will love it here.

S: You didn't mention feasts.

Edelweiss: You mean eating? We don't eat.

S: If you don't eat, how do you exist?

Edelweiss: We are spirits. Life here is totally clean. We have no waste. Plants, like animals, grow on love and need no chemicals or fertilizers to pollute the soil. Our dwellings are provided by God with no need for cutting down trees or digging unsightly holes for building materials.

S: And no newspapers to litter after reading them?

Edelweiss: Around Dewdrop and Rosebud, who needs them?

S: I want to ask Richard something.

Edelweiss: He's here, shifting impatiently as usual.

Richard: Thank you, ladies.

S: Richard: in the garden to people and animals understand all different languages?

Richard: We communicate easily with one another. The animals communicate with us and with each other telepathically. When I first arrived, a cantor from Russia spoke to me, and I understood every word. We had a long, interesting conversation.

S: You spoke so many languages.

Richard: The only time I wasn't talking or singing, I was sleeping! In my profession I met many from other countries of diverse customs, languages, religions, philosophies, appearances and life styles. It was a great pleasure and an education in itself, almost like reading an encyclopedia, only more fun. I loved it then, and love it now. We get together here in Spirit and trade many entertaining stories. We are never bored!

S: And if I am there with you some day, will I be accepted by all? You are so talented.

Richard: What do you mean, *if* you are here? Don't doubt it for a minute. They will love you, as I do. You will have much in common.

S: And my inability to sing?

Richard: I told you. I will teach you.

S: And I will teach a bullfrog to sing at the Metropolitan.

Richard: There are rules against bullfrogs at the opera.

S: Bigots! I'm shocked.

Richard: It will be a lot easier to teach you than your friend the frog.
S: When you hear me sing, you will hire the frog.
Richard: You will do fine.

◆   ◆   ◆

December 1999.

A Busy month! Just a few more days and we're in a new century—and millennium! The decorations are done, cards all mailed, the gifts are wrapped. The tree looks great hung with its ancient ornaments (sentiment over splendor). Rosie and Roger stayed in Ontario for a white Christmas, and Noel and I joined her friend Susan—like another daughter to me—for a cookout dinner at her house. I brought home a kitty bag for Mike. The squirrels even got an extra ration of peanuts. The last few days of the old millennium passed pleasantly and happily. Except for the very last day.

December 31, 1999.

S: My angels.
Edelweiss: We know what happened. We are so sorry.
S: My precious boy is dead. I was away from the house for a while, and when I returned he wasn't waiting for me out front as usual. It was getting dark, so I looked around for him. As I looked out the back door, I saw him lying on the ground nearby. I ran to him and saw that he had been torn to pieces by neighborhood dogs. All I could do at first was kneel over him, petting his torn little head and saying over and over, "I'm so sorry, so sorry." The dogs had dug out of their own confinement and came straight over here. He probably didn't think of running from them, as he knew them, and liked dogs. I ran next door and begged a cardboard box, and my neighbors kindly buried him in their

yard, as the ground over here is so hard. I hardly remember what I said or did, I was so distressed. He was the sweetest, gentlest cat I ever had, and was my spoiled baby boy. I can still see him coming from the back yard into the house through his pet door, waddling happily toward me as I sat in my favorite chair reading or watching TV.

Snowflake: Sarah, Mike will be here with us. We promise.

S: Thank God and bless you. I couldn't stand to think of his sweet life ending in that cold ground.

Snowflake. He's still sleeping after his transition, but will wake up here with us. He will be our special pet. We know you are grieving, but let me console you with the knowledge that he will be loved and cared for here.

S: Does Richard know?

Edelweiss: He's here.

S: Richard, when Mike awakens he will be so frightened.

Richard: He will be a little disoriented, but we will give him all the love and attention it takes to comfort him and put him at ease.

S: He won't understand.

Richard: You'd be surprised. Animals, like humans here in Spirit, are given a greater understanding of their surroundings and circumstances, and can communicate telepathically. He will soon adapt. He will miss you, and know you miss him.

S: You will spoil him? *Please!*

Richard, *Rotten,* as you put it. All our animals are pampered and loved and love us and each other very much. There are no hostilities or danger to them.

S: These thoughts will comfort me more than I can say. Richard, does Jericho know?

Richard: He cried real tears. They were close friends.

S: Will Jericho return here? He must be reluctant to be where there is no pet for him to love and play with.

Richard: He wants to be with you. He says you will get him another cat. We told him Mike was going to live with us and he could come and play with him. He says he will have two cats, and he is happy.

S: Last week I couldn't help but say "Merry Christmas" to Jericho. I surprised even me.

Richard: You would be glad if you knew how much it pleased him.

S: I know at times I will get angry at his shenanigans, but I will try to accept or at least tolerate him, as long as he behaves.

Richard: He likes and respects me (and my guillotine!). Threatening him usually works, with reprimands.

S: If I sleep tonight, I will wake up in the morning, the first day of the new millennium, and Mike won't be in the bed beside me. I miss him so much, and always will.

Richard: Yes, you will. I won't tell you not to grieve. But you must get another pet. You need it.

S: Mike can never be replaced.

Richard: Not to take his place, but to love in his memory, and be loved.

S: It will be such a comfort knowing he is in your loving care. Thank God for you and my angels.

Richard: You will see Mike again. We will all be together. Try to get some rest, and know that we love you and are looking out for you. You are very important to us.

S: Goodnight, love, and thank you.

Richard: Good night, my one and only love.

◆   ◆   ◆

January 1, 2000. Millennium!

Noel and I started out the next 1000 years having dinner with Peggy and Art at their lovely country home near Gainesville. They have no pets, as Peggy is allergic to animals, but were very sympathetic about my Mike. I needed to be around those I love. They are both very intelligent, as is Noel, and while the three of them discussed matters of universal importance, I listened and learned. When I got home, I called Richard and my angels.

S: My angels, I wanted to be with you on this first day of a new one thousand years.

Edelweiss: The Earth has come a long way since time began. But this is not the time to be philosophical. Did you have a nice day?

S: The new millennium began better for me than the last one ended. I haven't heard a peep out of Jericho, who is usually very active in his pestering pursuits.

Edelweiss: We told him not to bug you.

S: I'm sorry for him. But he will se Mike in Spirit. That's good, for both of them. Is Richard here?

All: Do cows moo?

S: Richard, do cows moo in Spirit?

Richard: Loud and clear. Not because they are hungry or need milking. They want attention. We spend a lot of time with our animals. They are spoiled.

S: In every garden?

Richard: yes, we can all have pets to care for and love, and St. Francis' Garden of Love has room for all who need a home. We can "adopt" animals from there on their arrival. Those who are there a while won't leave. They are happy there!

S: Wonderful! I get sick of the neglect or maltreatment of animals that happens in spite of responsible people who fight to protect them. No helpless creature should be abused, human or animal. It's inhuman. Richard, where do people who mistreat animals go when they pass into Spirit?

Richard: The same place as those who abuse humans go, and it's not fun. They have a large debt to pay. You know how sorry we are about Mike. He wouldn't want you to be unhappy.

S: I know, and I'm so glad I have you and my angels, and my daughters. I love you all.

Richard, We will let you know about Mike. Don't worry.

S: I will say good night. I'm bushed.

Richard: Bushed?

Edelweiss: She means she's tired.

Richard: Oh. Good night, love; sleep peacefully.

S: I'll dream of you.

◆　　　◆　　　◆

January 15, 2000.

Edelweiss: Somebody had a good time today!

S: Me! I attended a big mineral and gem show in Tampa. There are crafts and displays of every stone or gem mined in the ground or "fished" from the sea. I found a jade dragon for Noel, since she was born in the year of the dragon, and this first year of the millennium is a dragon year.

Edelweiss: A nice memento for her!

Rosebud: Nature's gifts are the most exquisite.

S: Do you have gemstones in Spirit?

Rosebud: Yes, they sparkle from the walls in our caves.

S: Do you wear them?

Rosebud: No, we leave them there for all to enjoy.

S: Ours are mined and created into jewelry and other artworks by our artisans.

Rosebud: God is our artisan! The stones of all colors glow and sparkle without cutting or polishing. Yours are beautiful. Earth craftsmen love to work with the joys and beauties of nature. They are inspired. Richard is here now.

Richard: You enjoyed your experience with the wonders of nature and man.

S: Many believe that each stone has a special meaning or gift, for example, amethyst for peace of mind, citrine for psychic involvement, garnet for happiness, ruby for strength, and the different colors of jade for wisdom, power, royalty, health, and the like. I have all these blessings and more, given to me by God through my five little jewels named Edelweiss, Rainbow, Dewdrop, Snowflake, and Rosebud. And by you, my ever vigilant and loving Spirit guide.

◆   ◆   ◆

21, January 2000.

S: Richard, don't look at me. I've been cleaning house.

Richard: What makes you think I am looking at your old work clothes and bare feet?

S: You *peeked*. Richard, can you see us here on Earth?

Richard: More like impressions, and sometimes visions telepathically, or, if you will, mentally. I even know what you looked like as a baby.

S: *Ugh!* I was a fat, ugly brat. I have never seen a picture of myself under the age of 16 smiling. I looked ready to kill.

Richard: In one of your pictures around the age of 7 you were trying to smile, keeping your mouth tightly closed because you had lost some baby teeth.

S: All I wanted for Christmas was my two front teeth.

Richard: You were cute! And I know exactly how you will be here with me in Spirit—young and beautiful.

S: And you will have your twinkling blue eyes, cute tummy-tum, charming personality and beautiful voice.

Richard: I'm listening raptly.

S: And your bossiness!

Richard: I care about you. You are not easy to look after. You think I am being overbearing when I want you to be happy.

S: Big kiss.

Richard: That's better.

S: Richard, I'll say nite-nite. Love you.

Richard: Big kiss to you, my love.

◆   ◆   ◆

January 24, 2000. Zora.

S: My angels!

Edelweiss: What is your new cat's name?

S: You knew! I wanted to surprise you. Her name is Zora. She's a big girl (not fat), dark gray and white. She used to live next door to me here, and was Mike's friend. The young couple who lived there, Kelly and Michael, left for the South Pacific with the Peace Corps and she was living with Kelly's mother Jean in the country. She wasn't very happy there, with three other cats in competition. She's a little nervous from moving around even though she's familiar with the surroundings, especially where the cat food dishes are located. I'm sure she'll adjust. Isn't she beautiful?

Snowflake: We all think so! What happened to her ear?

S: You mean the nick in her left ear? She was adopted in North Carolina. Every female cat there when spayed gets her ear snipped to show her "neutrality."

Snowflake: Oh, her lovely ear!

S: Kelly said it's the law.

Snowflake: Well, I think it's great to have animals neutered. There are too many little pets in your world without enough homes to go around. Zora doesn't seem to mind. We are all happy you have her. Here's Richard.

S: Richard, do you think Zora and Jericho will bond, as with Mike?

Richard: She can see him.

S: I'm sure he is wasting no time becoming evident. It's a talent with him. She is of a more aloof personality than Mike. It may take him time to bond. I didn't think at first that I would ever get another cat when Mike died, but I'm so glad I have her now. I think she misses Mike. She was looking all over the place, I think for him.

Richard: Definitely. Are you worried about the dogs?

S: They have been discouraged from digging out by an electric wire strung along the base of their fence, ready to "zap" them if they try to escape. It won't harm them, but they will get the message very soon and stay away from the fence! Zora is afraid of dogs, and would make for the nearest tree if any came around. I feel she will be all right.

◆   ◆   ◆

February 18, 2000.

Richard: Today is the first anniversary of your brother Morris' passing.

S: I don't feel he is dead. I have so many happy memories to hold.

Richard: He is very much alive. You will see him again.

S: And you and my angels.

Richard: Don't ever doubt that. Tell me about Zora.

S: She is adjusting beautifully. I'm sure she has befriended Pestiferous. She keeps leaning over into the space between the wall and the bed.

Richard: That's Jericho's den, under where you sleep.

S: I heard him last night, making crying sounds all the way through my pillow.

Richard: He wants your attention, even though his antics always get him into trouble.

S: Was he really crying?

Richard: Just acting. He only cries when he is in the doghouse (as he is now for his latest "crime") and he is not allowed to play with Mike on his visits here. He won't bother you for a while.

S: Until the next time. Acting, is he?

Richard: That's got to go. One ham in the family is enough.

S: One with a cute tummy-tum. What does Pestiferous look like?

Richard: You don't want to know, or you might see him, but he is a cute little rascal.

S: I'm beginning to learn all his haunts. Zora often goes into the bathroom behind the curtain. I've heard him tap on the wall over the tub. She also goes under the living room couch, which is covered, to the floor.

Richard: They nap there together. A great hideaway!

S: Zora has been getting into all the cabinets in both the kitchen and the bathroom. When I get home there are articles all over the floors. I swear she has fingers instead of toes on her paws. I had to change the location of her cat food.

Richard: Credit him with that. He has taught her to open the doors, so they can play hide and seek.

S: Well, I'm glad she has a friend. She doesn't have any neighbor animals to befriend, and I doubt if she wants any. I thought since she seems aloof, she might ignore Pestiferous.

Richard: They're thick as thieves.

S: That's a good description. They're both crooks. How's Mike?

Richard: Rotten spoiled. He spends more time on laps than he does on the ground.

S: Bless you all for caring about him.

Richard: He's happy you have Zora. He picked her out for you.

❖   ❖   ❖

March 4, 2000.

S: Anna Bess is in Punta Gorda vacationing. I visited her today at her apartment overlooking Charlotte Harbor. Somehow we are always drawn back to the beaches in Florida! It's called "sand in our shoes." The weather was beautiful. I especially enjoyed it knowing a drought will come soon.

Dewdrop: You will have plenty of water for yourselves and your plants.

Rosebud: You used to have lovely live plants in your house.

S: Once I was baby-siting a friend's kittens, who used potted plants as their kitty-litter. What a mess! Since then the real plants are outside and substitute fake ones inside for decorations. Did I ever tell you about the music-loving plants I had while living in Tampa?

Richard: I want to hear this!

S: I was living in a town house. The living room downstairs had a big sliding glass door that opened out upon a garden. Since my plants needed light, I placed two of them near the glass door, and one across the room under a lamp. Opposite all of them was my record player, much in use. One day I noticed the plants were leaning not toward the light but toward the record player. I turned them back toward the light, and in a day or two they were leaning again in the direction of the music. I favor classical music, but I also like the more modern or "pop" music, which I put on for a day or two. The plants continued to turn. Then I tried my Latino artists. The same thing happened. I worried about the lack of light, but the plants flourished! So I left them alone. Plants are sensitive! They love soft human voices, singing or talking, and different rhythms or musical interpretations. I must get some live plants back in the house. They will love your voice, Richard!

Richard: Plants in Spirit react as those on Earth—they grow happily and healthily with loving attention! Rosebud smiles when I kiss the beautiful white rose by the little bridge over a nearby stream.

S: What a happy rose that must be! You made so many hearts happy on Earth, and you are a light in Spirit!

◆   ◆   ◆

March 18, 2000.

S: Angels, do you remember what day this is?

Edelweiss: One year ago today there was a beautiful and touching military tribute to your brother at Arlington National Cemetery.

S: I still have not adjusted to being without him on Earth, but it is a great comfort to know he is well and happy, and that his family and all his friends will be with him again some day. Anna Bess can feel his presence even though she cannot see him. I have placed flowers every day on his "shrine" with a prayer candle. (I hope he doesn't mind the absence of the Mormon Tabernacle Choir and fireworks.) I want to talk to Richard about something.

Richard: You rang?

S: Richard, I've been getting strong feelings about writing a book. I don't know anything about writing. Are you haunting me about this?

Richard: I?

S: Don't act innocent. I know it's you.

Richard: Think about it. You have a lot of our communications documented. You can do it.

S: Richard, I'm not an author. I'm nobody. Who would publish it?

Richard: First, a list of characters, and descriptions.

S: You aren't listening.

Richard: Then…

S: Your bio?

Richard: Yours first.

S: I'm not as interesting as you. Nobody would get past my dull pages.

Richard: Then you can tell my story.

S: Well—some dialog, anecdotes, my interpretations—?

Richard: Good thinking.

S: I can't.

Richard: Just do it.

S: You do it, you're the artist. Writers are artists. Writing is an art.

Richard: You can. You must do it. I'll be right with you.

S: And keep Pestiferous from bothering me. You don't want cussing in your book.

Richard: Our book. I'm oiling the guillotine.

S: I love you.

Richard: And I you. Get busy!

S: *Ja wohl!* Good night, love. I'll try.

Richard: Good night, my one and only love.

◆   ◆   ◆

March 29, 2000.

Edelweiss: It's been a while, Sarah. We were afraid you wouldn't call us again, as you have been upset with us.

S: My daughters' father died. Although he never contacted them or sent them anything through the years, you indicated that he had arranged something for them when he passed.

Edelweiss: Sarah, don't hear only what you want to hear. You give people too much credit at times. Some people never change.

S: Noel and Rosie didn't care about any material things. We always took care of ourselves. If they could only remember their father with respect. Not that he would care, but they would. Maybe it's all for the best. I didn't want to raise the girls around any unpleasantness. He made fun of me, especially my figure, which everyone else considered good, including myself. I never told him about *his* short comings. And I do mean *short*.

Richard: You should pray for him.

S: Where is he?

Richard: You don't want to know. He is past history, and thank God for your deliverance from him, and for all your blessings. Now let's drop it.

S: You're right.

Richard: Remember that your angels and I are only God's servants. If you have perfect faith in Him, and trust us, His "media," it will be a lot easier for us.

When we communicate, take a deep breath, relax, and think peaceful things, and let us in. Not everything we tell you will be good. Most will be. You must accept our love and guidance, and believe wholeheartedly that we are working very hard in your interests, and *can* help you.

S: I promise. My life is happy. I like my job. Everyone is kind and helpful. I have in the past worked around many dreadfully unpleasant people. I'm so glad that is all past. Thank you for all your help.

Richard: You have always done your share of helping others, and not always with their appreciation. Your daughters are beautiful trophies of caring and love.

S: And now I have Zora! She is curled up on the bed beside me. The house, I might mention, has a new addition to the lizard population. I can't break her of the habit, and I can't always catch them, although I've rescued some.

Richard: She's in hog heaven. The lizards are gifts to you.

S: She can't catch the squirrels.

Richard: They are too fast for her.

S: Now I'm getting drowsy.

Richard: Go to sleep, love.

◆   ◆   ◆

April, 2000. Drought.

S: I am fossilized.

Edelweiss: You aren't suffering. You have and will have plenty of water.

S: When it rains I feel a peace and well being—as long as it isn't destructive.

Edelweiss: You have been very quiet during this Lenten period.

S: Yes, it's a time of meditation and reflection on one's life and what we accomplish to deserve all our blessings. Some people "give up" certain things they enjoy to remind them how it would be without God's love and gifts to us. I don't give up anything. If I gave up ice cream or candy I would probably eat them anyway. Rather than take away, I add in prayer and acts of charity to others, and vow to continue these acts when Lent ends.

Snowflake: But you always do for others.

S: Not enough. Every one of us is needed and should do everything possible to make this world a better place to live in. I hope to merit being with you some day.

Rosebud: Here's Richard. He will ask you to give up something.

S: I wonder what?

Richard: Cussing.

S: I'm trying.

Richard: Jericho told me what you called him.

S: The little bandit awakened me last night by banging on the wall over my head. It sounded like the house was being bombed. I nearly jumped out of my skin.

Richard: He's in the doghouse. He can't play with Mike, and he is afraid of the guillotine.

S: Why does he keep misbehaving when he knows he'll catch it?

Richard: He's just a big kid, and you know that once in a while he can't resist a little mischief.

S: How can he do noisy things when he doesn't even have a body or physical means?

Richard: A manifestation of energy through spirit control. If he were evil, he could fling you high and hard against the wall.

S: In what spirit category is Jericho, to have such powers?

Richard: He is an imp.

S: Richard, imps are *demons!*

Richard: He is not evil.

S: A demon? How not evil?

Richard: Jericho came to Earth with others of his kind on a mission of evil mischief. He saw a cat and was totally smitten. When the "leader" told him he couldn't have one, he deserted the pack and wandered about in search of a home with a cat, and chose you and Mike.

S: It must mean something that Mike loved him, as does Zora.

Richard: When you complained to me about him, I sent Snowflake to fetch him. When I talked to him about his behavior, fortunately he bonded with me. Imps want to be guided and monitored. They love attention and know how to get it. This you must consider, Sarah. If a holy spirit such as Lucifer, God's favorite and most beautiful angel, turned away from Him to be an evil king instead of a holy follower, then why can't the opposite happen? For all his mischievous antics, Jericho wants to follow the righteous. He loves you and protects you. He will be monitored and disciplined. But the bottom line is that you are stuck with him. Please try to understand and encourage his positive action.

S: Why didn't he help Mike when those dogs came into the yard and killed him?

Richard: When he entered your house, he was bound inside. He can come to us in Spirit in a split second, but you have to permit his presence outside where you live. Just tell him it's all right.

S: Right—but I hope he doesn't freak out my neighbors, and I don't want him materializing to me or anyone else!

Richard: He won't.

S: Richard, while we're on the subject of spirits, tell me about ghosts. Do they inhabit one place to haunt, or wander? Are some evil and some good? Why are they earthbound? Have they chosen to stay here, or forbidden to enter through the Light? Are they condemned?

Richard: Ghosts are really pathetic creatures who desperately need help. Some refuse to leave Earth, insisting they still belong there. Some do not accept that they are no longer alive in human form. There are houses or buildings haunted by a spirit who either lived there or suffered a traumatic experience on that property. These are generally harmless, but frighten those who may see or hear them. No one is forbidden to enter Spirit through the Light, but some don't want to face the discipline they know awaits them. This is extremely unfortunate. The reconciliation period may last a while, but it leads to eternal happiness. There are vagabond spirits who seek on Earth what they never accomplished in life. In spirit form as in human, they are "losers" who never listened to anyone who tried to help them in any way, and may never do so. Please pray for all those poor creatures. When you are aware of one of these unfortunate beings, send an angel to save him or her.

S: I will send Snowflake.

Richard: She will go.

S: Are poltergeists and banshees ghosts?

Richard: No, just noisy nuisances. They cannot penetrate angel protection. They don't even have any kind of form, just some of old Mr. Scratch's contrivances. Like him, they are a lot of hot air. People, get in touch with your angels. If you don't think you have an angel band, there is no problem getting one. All you have to do is ask. They will lead you to the self-confidence and energy you need to achieve what you want on this Earth.

S: And God bless you all. Amen.

Richard: Contact with the Spirit world is normal and healthy, and most rewarding to both sides. Our good spirits are very anxious and ready to help those left behind on Earth.

Some think it is phony or weird. It is neither. How could a loving God ever be so cruel as to cut us off from loved ones so abruptly and brutally? Our beloved ones who precede us into Spirit love us and miss us. They want to keep in touch, and to help and guide us with their love and prayers. We will see each other again, in a beautiful garden put there for us by God.

One on Earth who has not repented for his sins must atone in Spirit. The methods imposed vary for each individual. Imagine a cold-blooded criminal made to watch himself committing all the horrors he has imposed on humanity, millions of times, and having to face them and all their broken-hearted loved ones, all who suffered his cruelty. Having to watch himself murder, rape, rob, cheat, steal, and all the other foul deeds does not make him happy he did those things. He is shown visions of happy spirits in their own little Paradises, and longs for their happiness and peace. After hundreds—or thousands—of eons he has cried millions of tears. He can't believe what a fool he was, and begs for another chance at happiness. He is counseled lengthily by angels. They decide when he is given this "chance," which may be eventual admittance to a colony with a clean slate, or rebirth on Earth with the opportunity to live a decent, productive life. If he goofs on this one, for eternity he will be a lonely, miserable spirit, with the greatest punishment of all: to face eternity without the Presence of God, worse than any raging Hell fires!

S: What about the devil?

Richard: If we live right, he cannot harm us. He cannot penetrate the protective shield of righteousness. He preys on selfish, uncaring people. He doesn't own anyone. All he can do is force us, by our own weakness, to spend much time in reparation for our sins. God controls that, not Mr. Scratch.

S: So I'd better stop the bad words.

Richard: Right. If you need spiritual help, choose wisely. There are many ministers of every faith and competent metaphysicians who are happy to help us with problems and assisting with our contacts through the Light. Use careful judgment distinguishing between the ethical and the fake.

S: Speaking of fakes, just for fun a friend and I stopped at a roadside fortune teller some time ago. Immediately she started trying to bilk me.

She said there was a handsome man very interested in me but was shy, and if I gave her fifty dollars she would cast a spell and bring him to me. I told her, "I'll give you fifty dollars to keep him away!"

Richard: I wonder who the poor guy was.

S: You know good and well there was no guy. Besides, if he didn't have the guts to declare himself, and makes me pay fifty dollars to get him, the heck with him!

Richard: I wish I'd been there. But seriously, and with great emphasis, let me warn you about Ouija boards. If you believe that spirits can really enter through the board, they will, and not always the ones you summoned. Stay away from spells and magic.

S: Your advice will be helpful to many.

◆   ◆   ◆

April 18, 2000.

Edelweiss: Someone is having a bad day.

S: Growl! Rrrr!.

Edelweiss: You've got fullmoonitis.

S: Maybe I should've checked the lunar calendar today. The drought is awful, I can't concentrate on Richard's book, and a dead tree just fell in my yard. I love Richard, but he has given me a task of which I don't feel capable.

Edelweiss: That's your problem right there. Don't say you can't do something, or you won't. Always be optimistic!

S: May I talk to Richard?

Richard: I'm here.

S: Don't say anything.

Richard? Where are you, Richard? Speak to me.

Richard: You said not to say anything.

S: You're going to fuss at me about the book.

Richard: I'm not. Now, relax, take a deep breath, and think nice.

S: You haven't changed in your determination since your Earth days.

Richard: I wouldn't get anywhere with you if I had. Don't be your own worst enemy. No one can stop you if you believe in yourself.

S: As you did, and do.

Richard: If I didn't believe in myself, who would?

S: Did you ever cuss?

Richard: I decline to answer.

S: Are you taking the Fifth Amendment?

Richard: What is that?

S: In a court of justice, a witness may refuse to answer a question that may tend to incriminate him if he answers it.

Richard: I'm home safe. You haven't worked on our book.

S: You promised to help me. I'm uninspired.

Richard: I can't put the pen in your hand. If you don't have modern devices like computers or typewriters, write it by hand and have someone type it for you.

S: Are you sure people won't think it's weird?

Richard: I've seen stranger things in print. People love the metaphysical, if that's what our relationship is. Besides, weird is different. I don't mind being a little weird, do you?

S: Weird, ha! You are disgustingly normal. Everything you have ever done has been clean and fair and productive. I can't find a single bit of scandal or even gossip about you.

Richard: Did you look for it?

S: No, but if it had been there, I would have found it.

Richard: You haven't done badly yourself.

E: Especially since you and my angels have been watching over me. I listened to your operetta "Old Chelsea" today. Besides being a great singer, you're an excellent composer. I especially liked the song "My Heart and I" Richard, why is the heart the symbol of love? I've always wondered. It's an organ of the body like many other vital processes.

Richard: How would it sound if I sang, "We are in love with you, my liver and I?"

S: Or, "I love you with all my spleen."

Richard: If young people could hear us, they might be discouraged from falling in love. The heart is the center of activity in the body that is strongly affected by the emotions, and therefore it represents love. Unfortunately, strong emotions of any kind can affect it also, and cause illness.

S: Unrequited love?

Richard: Or hatred.

S: Or both. I have seen love turned into hatred and beauty into evil. Even religions warring against each other in the Name of God. Churches of all sects are supposed to teach us to be kind and gentle.

Richard: God is more concerned about our behavior out of church than in. Combining attendance in church and living according to its tenets pleases Him immensely.

S: I know of religious people who live genuinely good lives, one example being the sweet Sisters of the Holy Name Monastery, who taught me as a teenager. I'll never forget the values I learned from them. God bless and keep them. There are, however, other religious institutions which do not merit their names. If you were looking for the nastiest people on earth, you might check out the department heads of one institution of higher learning. You wouldn't be a bit disappointed. You cup would runneth over.

Richard: Don't dwell on the faults of others! Work on your own and let God handle the others. Don't hate anyone. Hate is doing your enemies a favor. They are rationalizing and sanctifying their actions—they think—by incurring your resentment. Wasn't it Jesus who said the most effective way to treat those who offend you is to be kind to them and bless them? You have defeated them by nullifying their intentions. Those with swastikas on their uniforms and death's heads on their caps hated me because I was famous and part Jewish.

Instead of returning their hatred, I kept in my mind all those friends who loved, inspired and strengthened me. In the end, who won?

S: You did. But you had the good sense to leave continental Europe before they caught up with you. What about all those poor souls the Nazis murdered?

Richard: They have been rewarded a million fold for their suffering, dwelling in a beautiful home, happy for all eternity. Remember what I said about atonement. It will be many eons, if ever, before those who persecuted and murdered innocent men, women and children will be admitted to Paradise.

◆   ◆   ◆

Easter Day, 2000.

S: Happy Easter! I can't wait to hear about your Resurrection celebration in the presence of Our Lord Jesus.

Edelweiss: He was here! Today's topic was of His deep love and concern for the young on Earth.

Every country boasts of its natural resources. One may be gold, another oil, or gems, or silver, or other things. Jesus says that the greatest resource of any country is its youth. The children of today are the responsible citizens and leaders of tomorrow. Most are fine young people, carefully taught and given good examples by their parents, but not always! There is the danger of kids today growing up too fast, with too many liberties—that they resent when given, even though they demanded them! Even some of the very young have their own computers, and when not using these are watching television (some of which is pretty graphic) or renting violent movies. These are keeping them quiet while their parents are occupied with their business or social lives. Our modern growth in technology is conducive to great advancement in their learning, but does not take the place of Mom and Dad. The greatest gifts of a parent to a child are a shining example of good character, and the three big "A" words: Affection, Attention, and Approval. Try these gifts. They work every time! This may sound "corny" to you, and if you want to call Jesus "corny," go to it.

Now, I'll give you *my* three cents' worth! You need to put a harness on the Internet. It's getting completely out of control. Your "freedoms" are ruining the true meaning of freedom. "Freedom of the press" is a pain in the go-go. Whatever happened to freedom of privacy? Celebrities who have worked hard to attain their success are afraid even to go to the bathroom unless there are high fences around their property with guards or dogs, or both, like a penitentiary. Without this protection, a picture of a celebrity in the bathroom would appear on the front page of every tabloid in business. Another could appear seemingly jaybird naked on the computer screen, with his or her face only, but imposed on the body of some sleaze who gladly took pay for embarrassing someone else. Freedom, right?

Agencies, even government files, can be accessible to clever computer hacks. You're not going to rid the Internet of sexual harassment and filth until you put the brakes on the possibilities given by your "freedoms."

S: Whew! Edelweiss, you know how to get tough!

Edelweiss: In your world, I earned a black belt in mouth karate.

S: You don't swear, though.

Edelweiss: It's not cool.

Richard: What's a "go-go?"

Edelweiss: It's creole for "seat."

Richard: Oh. I think I've heard Jericho use that term.

S: He picked it up when I told Zora to get her go-go off the table.

Richard: Did you hear Edelweiss say cussing is not cool?

S: I think you're cool.

Richard: Did you have a nice Easter?

S: A big traditional dinner with some of my favorite family—Noel, Art and Peggy. Rosie and Roger spend Easter in Canada. The angels told me about Jesus' visit. I can't imagine ever really being with him in person.

Richard: you will. You will be perfectly at ease with him!

◆   ◆   ◆

April 30, 2000.

Snowflake:
We know Zora is beside you sleeping peacefully. She loves you and feels secure.

S: She is a joy—most of the time! Tonight she was in the bathroom romping around with Pestiferous, almost tearing the curtains down!

Snowflake: He likes the tub.

S: I wish you could keep him out of it. When I take a shower, I can feel spook eyes on me. That, however, is not what I came to you about this evening. I need your advice about the book.

Dewdrop: Write humorously. You can make lovable fun of all of us. We want the world to know that we in Spirit don't go around with long faces and holier-than-thou attitudes. We love to laugh! Laughter is one of God's blessings to us.

S: I wouldn't make fun of you, but we have laughed together and cried together and I would like to tell everything about our wonderful relationship and how real and lovable and funny you are! Rosebud, how do you and Dewdrop get all of your information, or as Jesus puts it, your "latest?"

Richard: By being nosy.

S: Ignore him, Rosebud. Do you have special powers in that respect?

Richard: "Busybodies, Inc." is an intergalactic chain of communication satellites.

Rosebud: We are in contact with many other colonies in Spirit and on Earth.

Dewdrop: Richard loves to tease us! Our contacts are varied but we can—and do—tune in on your television broadcasts.

Richard: And the tabloids. Especially gossip.

Rosebud: I don't hear anyone complaining! It gets awfully quiet here when we report, everyone leaning to listen with big rabbit ears.

S: Don't stop! You are providing a valuable service. Now, I have a matter for Richard about Pestiferous.

Richard: I know. He is in the doghouse.

S: He always waits until I am sleeping peacefully to pull his worst little tricks. I was awakened last night by what sounded like snoring. Did I awaken myself snoring? I wondered. Then I heard it again. Where does he get his bright ideas?

Richard: He thinks he is Mr. Funny Man. He is crying because we wont let him play with Mike.

S: Can you keep him and Zora out of my bathtub? Tell him also he can't play with Zora. I wish she would bite him. Kiss my Mike for me. I miss him a lot. I'm so glad he's with you and the angels.

Richard: You will see him and many others here one day.

S: And you and the angels.

Richard: Now you believe!

◆   ◆   ◆

May 7, 2000.

Edelweiss: You finally started the book!

S: Is it going all right?

Richard: I especially like the parts where you extol my virtues and talents.

S: You big ham, Richard.

Richard: I admit it.

S: Pestiferous has been quiet lately but for some light tapping on the glass objects in the nick-nack shelves. This is at least a change for the better from the wall bangings.

Richard: He says it's more musical.

S: If I could see him, I'd throw one at him.

Richard: It wouldn't do any good. After a stern lecture, he'll be good for a while.

S: Would you tell him to at least limit his activities to daylight hours?

Richard: It's more fun in the dark, when you're asleep. You wouldn't expect a self-respecting spook to perform in the daytime, would you?

S: Yes, and he does. He's on duty 24 hours a day, only he's worse at night. Angels, where is rain? We need it spiritually and physically. All my poor weeds are dead.

Edelweiss: Speaking of physical needs, you spent the night in the hospital.

S: No big deal, just needed a prescription change. If I'd had some games to play, I'd have challenged Snowflake to a game of checkers.

Snowflake: I was there. Be careful. I'm good at checkers.

S: You're on, when I get there!

Richard: Just don't get rambunctious. Get plenty of rest.

S: I hate rest. It bores me. Anyway, you and the angels look after me so well, I'm not afraid of anything. I love all of you.

◆   ◆   ◆

May 16, 2000.

S: I believe we have a birthday boy.

Edelweiss: Yes, he's here, anxiously awaiting you.

S: Happy birthday, my love.

Richard. Thank you for the flowers. They are lovely.

S: I am listening to your records. Some day I will hear you sing to me.

Richard: Every time you hear my voice, I am singing to you.

S: And I love it.

Richard: Your Mike is here with me. He is spoiled and happy!

S: He knows he is blessed. Jericho is behaving fairly well. He and Zora are getting along fine—too fine, if you ask me. I cussed at Pestiferous recently for wall tapping at 3 a.m.

Richard: I told him to cool it. I don't want him bothering you.

S: You are learning "jive talk."

Richard: Edelweiss is a bad influence on me.

S: I will light a candle tonight and place it by your picture and the flowers. It will represent my love for you.

Richard: I hope it burns as brightly as mine for you.

S: Happy birthday and a peaceful good night, my sweet spirit.

Richard: Good night, my one and only love.

◆   ◆   ◆

May 25, 2000.

Edelweiss: You don't seem your usual bright and cheery self.

S: I feel like a fossil in the middle of the Gobi Desert. When will it rain? The Earth is shrinking.

Edelweiss: Cheer up. Watch the TV weather reports. We'll have your rain. After that, look out for the hurricane season. Better get busy writing. As Snuffy says, "Time's a-wastin'!"

Snowflake: Snuffy?

Rosebud: A cartoon character. We read the *Tribune*.

S: How is Noel doing in Spain?

Rosebud: Having a great time at all the parties and celebrations of her goddaughter's wedding in Madrid.

S: Please watch over her. I'm nervous about plane flights these days.

Rosebud: She will be fine. Richard is here.

Richard: Time's a-wastin'! You wouldn't watch my movie tonight. You put on "Land of Smiles" and then soon took it off.

S: My eyes were very tired. I see you every minute in my mind and heart. Or, as you so poetically suggested, in my liver.

Richard: You're not going to forget that.

S: Thankfully, Pestiferous has been quiet. The other day, I was sitting peacefully in my favorite chair watching TV, and happened to glance over toward the video shelf, against which a huge black snake was comfortably coiled. At first I froze, but then I realized this must be one of Zora's old friends from where she lived next door. "Clarissa," as I called the then small, harmless snake, lived among the hedges dining on insects. Zora was always after her, and I had to rescue her several times from snatching paws. She now had finally captured Clarissa, all 2½ feet of her! I picked her up and took her to a nearby field. As I carried her, she looked up at me and stuck out her little forked tongue. I don't know if she was making a face at me, or trying to figure out what I was. She slithered happily off into the woods. We haven't seen her since. Tonight I rescued a baby bird in the house. I put it over the fence where its parents can tend to it. I hope Zora leaves it alone.

Richard: These "critters" are gifts to you. She doesn't have money to buy you presents, and this is her way to show appreciation. Don't worry about the little guy. Bird parents are very protective. Zora will get a good pecking if she tries again.

S: Good! Richard, I am going to a flea market in Monday, Memorial Day.

Richard: Flea market?

S: They don't sell fleas there. It's an open market where practically everything old and new man ever created can be found.

Richard: In Europe we had these outdoor markets, but mostly foodstuffs and new items like crafts or trinkets. They were fun, as yours are.

S: And please lobby for me for rain.

Richard: What's that?

S: When congress is in session, those who are interested in special causes attend, to try to convince lawmakers to pass legislation for their interests. It's called "lobbying." Only do it in Spirit, in prayer, not in Washington, or you'll freak out the politicians.

Richard: Some of them need it.

S: I love you! Good night.

Richard, Good night, love. Stay out of the hospital.

◆   ◆   ◆

End of June, 2000.

S: What a beautiful month this has been! Everybody well, rain, everything going right rain, no hurricanes, rain. And *rain!*

Edelweiss: You haven't contacted us in a few days.

S: I know you are with me, but you like the written contact. I've been doing some work on the book. Richard?

Richard: (silence)

S: Richard? You aren't speaking? Richard? Hell-ll-ooo!

Richard: I'm pouting.

S: Talk to me please. I need some advice from you.

Richard: How, if you don't contact us? We think you don't need us when you don't call.

S: You know better than that. About the book…

Richard: What book?

S: *Pleease?*

Richard: You don't talk enough about yourself.

S: Do you want to bore people? Doctors will prescribe it for insomnia patients.

Richard: Talk more about your marriages.

S: Big snore. No way! Besides, you don't talk about yours. What if I got there and she were with you? You were happy.

Richard: We were. That's past history. She is with someone else now in Spirit, and very contented. I'm so happy to have you, and always will be. You are my only love. You are *mine*. I will never let you go.

S: I don't want you to, but sometimes you seem too good to be true. As the old saying goes, "If something seems too good to be true, it probably is."

Richard: You Americans and your sayings.

S: I would love you even if you didn't know I exist. Your Garden of Song must be so beautiful. If I were to hear the names of some of your friends there, would I recognize them?

Richard: You would. We have welcomed many great singers and artists. I will not mention any out of respect for their families.

S: Please don't be angry with me.

Richard: Stay in contact. I want things written down for your manuscript. Good night, now, love.

S: Good night, my sexy phantom.

◆   ◆   ◆

July 4, 2000.

S: The flags are waving for our independence! I have a big bow in red, white and blue on my front door.

Richard: Your community is big on decorating for each holiday, according to Rosebud and Dewdrop.

S: You should see the St. Charles, a darling little inn around the corner from my house. On holidays, people love to see their decorations. Before all the big roads and interstates were constructed, it was a popular little hotel for travelers passing this way. It was bought and renovated by a young couple. Now they have everything out there except Washington crossing the Delaware. Waving prominently in the front is a big American flag, of course! You should see their Halloween decorations.

Richard: Spare me. I'm sure they're wonderful, but as I told you, I'm afraid of ghosts.

S: It hasn't changed much here since I was a schoolgirl. Some new houses and businesses, but in all, the same quiet, restful atmosphere, among pine and oak woods, and many citrus groves. The old St. Anthony Church, in which I graduated from Holy Name Academy, and the park in the center of town are still the same. Usually the hills and fields and roadsides are covered with wild phlox of many colors in spring, a spectacle that dates back a century. This year, because of the drought, the flowers didn't even come up;. When I had my Maisie I had permission form the sisters at Holy Name to let her run on the beautiful grounds and swim in Lake Jovita. Playful otters tried to intercept her as she swam for the sticks I tossed in the water, but she growled at them to stay away. A big field that was once the nesting place in the spring for meadowlarks is now a ball park for the Little League players. I miss the birds, but it's great for the kids.

Richard: You haven't talked about your job.

S: I work part-time at Career Central in Dade City doing mostly interpreting and assigned clerical duties. It's great to see people of all ages getting job training and subsequent employment. It's pleasant working there, a welcome change from some of the jobs I've had in this area.

Richard, I hear thunder. Music to my ears! Zora has taken over Mike's old cowering place under the couch. There is something to tell you, about the dogs that killed Mike. Following an unfortunate incident, they were taken away. That's all I know. I felt sorry, as everyone loves his pets, but sometimes things happen for the best.

Richard: They are in a special section of St. Francis' garden. They will be trained to love and obey before they can move freely and happily among the others there.

S: I'm glad they are given a chance.

Richard: Right now your Mike is on Snowflake's lap.

S: I wish animals on Earth could have angels' laps to sleep on sometimes.

Richard: What makes you think they don't? It happens. In the meantime, Jericho confessed his latest felony. It's doghouse time.

S: Good. I was awakened last night by the loud hissing and spitting that cats make when angry or threatened. I turned on the bedside lamp and saw only Zora lying quietly beside me.

Richard: He was trying to drum up a little excitement by starting a ruckus with her.

S: She complacently ignored him. What will he think of next?

Richard: Mike is off limits, and I threatened him with the guillotine.

S: Is he still falling for that one?

Richard: You know I can be very serious. I'm not an actor for nothing.

S: Do the angels know the pest?

Richard: They think he's cute. Snowflake thinks I'm too harsh with him.

S: She knows he can get out of hand if not disciplined.

Richard: I like the book, especially the parts about how great I am.

S: Tell me seriously, how is it going?

Richard: On the right track!

◆   ◆   ◆

August 18, 2000.

Snowflake: Do we hear sneezing?

S: I'm coming down with something. Yuk!

Snowflake: Hit the Vitamin C bottle.

S: The news around the world is so sad. Fires, floods, political unrest, accidents, and there is a submarine lying on the floor of the

Dead Sea with a brave crew aboard. I'm praying hard for their rescue. Imagine what the loved ones of those men are going through. Blessed Mother will surely hear and answer our prayers.

Edelweiss: We are all praying for those brave men. But remember this, Sarah. Our prayers never go unanswered, regardless of what happens. There are always rewards. Be comforted.

S: Is Richard here?

All: Do cows moo?

S: Richard, I feel lousy.

Richard: You have lice?

Edelweiss: She means she doesn't feel well.

Richard: I know. Snowflake will take care of you. She knows how much you mean to me.

S: And you to me. Please don't ever change.

Richard: Never.

S: I'm seeing school buses lately. Autumn is near! I love seeing the children getting their education.

Richard: You made a good education,. You were wise to achieve it.

S: Yes, though I had material things, I wanted to ensure my future. One never knows what will happen in this life. Girls may get married after school and never work, preferring family life at home with the kids. However, it doesn't hurt for husbands to know that their wives are perfectly capable of taking care of themselves—and the children!—should the necessity occur. These men will not take their wives for granted. Several friends I had in high school married without pursuing college or professional training. After several children, there wasn't much they could do about their husbands' "whims" and abuses. Thank God I never subjected myself to that kind of situation, and I trained both of my daughters to think wisely and realistically along those lines. Both are very happy. I don't mean to imply that all men are abusive (some *women* are!), but there's no harm in a little insurance called "independence." One of those husbands I mentioned told his wife, and mother of five kids, that he would disappear into South

America if she divorced him, and asked how she planned to support *her* children?

I was never the "marrying kind" anyway. I always took care of my daughters and myself, as many others do. The only thing, I aver, that a woman can't do that a man can involves the way he goes to the bathroom. I could put that in a more graphic way, but I will contain myself on this one!

Richard: I was holding my breath! What resulted with your friends' unhappy marriages?

S: Their feeling sorry for themselves. I have no compassion for self-pity. Let them get off their butts and get a…. life. They destroy themselves and frequently those around them, who may feel obliged to cater to the miserable self-pitier instead of living their own lives freely and happily. It's a scam, and I refuse to be a part of it in any way.

Richard: Your advice to young women is excellent. I myself had no higher education.

S: Are you kidding? With your high level of intelligence, wisdom, guts and determination, and most of all your great inherent talent, all promoting a successful career, I would rate your education the highest. Certainly higher than mine!

Richard: My parents taught me to read and write before I was school age. I had no trouble in learning, though I attended many schools. You said you attended foreign schools.

S: Cuba and México. While I was a student of the university of Havana in 1946, there was a very loud and politically active young law student named Fidel Castro. I said to myself that he will either end up in front of a firing squad or one day become president of Cuba.

Visiting my uncle and family in eastern Cuba, I heard of a witch nearby known for her psychic readings and spell-casting. Maria's appearance alone would put the fear of God—or the devil—in anyone. Over six feet tall, weighing around 300 pounds, with strong, bony features, she "read" by gazing intently into a glass of clear water. I was told I would have a happy, eventful life and two beautiful daughters, but that I would have an earth-shattering experience in my future. I'll say! In 1965 on a tour of México we experienced a 6.7 earthquake. Outside of scaring the daylights out of us, there were no injuries.

Anyway, back to Cuba: I've got to tell this one. (Always a good story there.) My uncle liked to tell about his experiences amid all the revolutions and political riots so prevalent there. One of his favorites concerned the overthrow of the dictator Machado by General Batista's men in the thirties. One of Machado's henchmen owned a palatial mansion in Santiago de Cuba, with a magnificent wrought-iron gateway from which the owner's head swung majestically. Every time Uncle Julien told this story, I'd day to myself, "He's told that one so many times he's believing it himself." Not long ago, I found a book by Desi Arnaz, whose father was employed by the Machado government, and who fortunately escaped with his family to the U. S. In his book, Arnaz described this gateway ornament exactly as my uncle had.

Edelweiss: I missed that one.

S: The dictatorship under Batista wasn't much better, and then after various Cuban presidents, along came Castro. My uncle's next door neighbor, a young man I danced with once at a party, was executed by Castro for terrorism. It seems that this young man had been active all along in every regime, bombing away determinedly for his "cause." Cause, my foot! Terrorism has no cause except killing and destroying, behind the mask of a "cause." Uncle Julien always managed to stay out of trouble. His motto was "Mind your own business in Cuba, and you'll survive."

The Adventures of Edelweiss

Edelweiss' comment, "I missed that one," intrigued me, reminding me that she had a lot of experience on Earth worth hearing about.

Edelweiss: You rang?

S: you haven't told me of your experiences on Earth as an invisible spectator.

Edelweiss: I thought you would never ask.

S: Tell me about what interested you most, and your impressions.

Edelweiss: I have visited many places on Earth in order to understand the people and their customs. Every country has its beauties of nature, interesting people and charming customs. I decided, however, in my educational pursuits, to "major" in America.

S: Why us?

Edelweiss: You have roller coasters!

S: Edelweiss, do the Seraphim know you were zooming around on rides when you were supposed to be working?

Edelweiss: All work and no play make Edelweiss a dull angel. Anyway, I wanted to be a guardian angel, and North Americans are fun and have great amusement parks.

S: I'm glad you came. Go on.

Edelweiss: The land of your [French] ancestors' first settlement in America, Acadia, known now as Nova Scotia in Canada, is where I started my journey.

S: Students who have read "Evangeline" by Longfellow know something of its history. Rosie brought me an Acadian flag, not now a valid banner but a memorial tribute to Acadia's rich past. It is basically the French tricolor, blue, white and red with a gold star in the upper left corner. It's beautiful.

Edelweiss: the people in that area are hardworking, friendly and good natured. I understood the French they still speak there. It's a beautiful language. You studied French, Sarah. You need to find someone to converse with in that language.

S: My mother and aunt spoke French when they didn't want us kids to understand their "adult talk." I understood it anyway.

Edelweiss: As I passed over Basin Minas from where the conquering British shipped out the French inhabitants…

S: For remaining loyal to France!

Edelweiss:…I saw a man and his small son fishing in the Bay of Fundy. The father had helped his son bait the hook hanging from his little pole and the child waited excitedly for a fish to tug at the line.

Time passed, and I wanted to put one on the hook for him, but children have to learn for themselves. Then the pole started bobbing and lo! with his father standing by, he pulled in a nice fish. It was a great moment for the little boy—he did it all by himself! A peaceful, happy scene.

S: Then?

Edelweiss: On to New York! How many angels can say they have flown over the Statue of Liberty?

S: Tell me about your favorite "sport."

Edelweiss: I *had* to see Coney Island. I felt guilty getting on the roller coaster without a ticket. I found an empty seat up front, for the ride of my life. I still can't figure out how it stayed on the track, going so fast, but I'm no engineer.

S: What was your reaction?

Edelweiss: Wheee!

S: You're braver than I am.

Edelweiss: I smelled so many wonderful things!

S: If you don't eat, how can you smell?

Edelweiss: If I didn't, how could I smell a rose?

S: Your point. Go on.

Edelweiss: Never a dull moment in New York! While going down a street in Manhattan, I saw people out early walking their dogs. Their owners were a bit puzzled by their pets' behavior as I got near. The dogs were looking up at me, joyfully wagging their tails. Wouldn't their owners have freaked out if they had known their pets were greeting an angel!

S: There was at one time an amusing TV program about people and animals. One segment featured dogs' tails wagging to music matching the rhythm of the wag.

Edelweiss: I got three waltzes, two polkas and a march.

S: You didn't miss a zoo, I'm sure!

Edelweiss: The Bronx. They have wonderful spacious environments for the animals, comparable to their natural habitats. So much better than cages!

S: Which were your favorites?

Edelweiss: All. The animals are situated of course out of the reach of visitors (Ha, ha). A mama tiger rolled over on her back when I scratched her tummy. She had two cubs, the female being the more aggressive. The little male finally got tired of her roughhousing and gave her a good swat with his paw. I loved the gorillas, who are by nature gentle and shy. A huge silverback reached out to touch me, trying to figure out what I was! There were many children there, listening to guides lecturing them about the animals. What a great idea! I had a lot of fun, and was so happy that people today are learning to have more respect and consideration for animals as well as for their fellow humans. We have a long way to go, but the Circle of Harmony, symbolizing the precious relationship that flows from God and His angels and spirits to man and his environment, and his love and responsibility for all creatures and nature, all are offered up to our loving Lord to complete a perfect circle. Let's all work and pray that your future generations will feel the power and act accordingly with these blessings to bring peace upon your beloved Earth and complete a perfect Circle of Harmony.

S: Central Park?

Edelweiss: It's like an oasis viewed from above, in the midst of a huge steel and concrete empire! Some kids were bicycling.

S: I'll be surprised if you didn't get on a bike.

Edelweiss: Oh, sure. Like a bicycle driving around by itself. There are some temptations I must pass on. I floated to the top of the Empire State Building. Soon the light of the city illuminated the clear, beautiful night. I marveled at the genius of man's creativity. If God had not given men the freedom of thought and action, all this would not have been possible. Would that God's great gifts to mankind would all be channeled into positive energy! There is no place in all your world in which I found no natural beauty in conjunction with the adaptable and enterprising people and animals.

S: Enterprising *animals*?

Edelweiss: Absolutely, especially in places still uninhabited by humans—and these are diminishing! I watched a beaver family in their ingenious, strongly built home in a deep, dammed-off pool. What a construction!

S: But we have wonderful machines.

Edelweiss: Let's see you cut down a tree with your teeth. Different animals and birds work wonders building the most comfortable, safe homes to accommodate their families. Animal parents are attentive and protective. In the beaver home I played with three fat, cuddly babies while the parents were out foraging for food.

S: How did you like our West?

Edelweiss: The deserts are wondrous. Aptly named, the Painted Desert changes colors at various times of day. Not even a painting by a great artist can capture the feeling of actually being there to witness its glory. Part of the desert has great trees that have fallen and turned to stone!

S: The Petrified Forest. Edelweiss, do you know how old those trees are? Millions of years.

Edelweiss: That's a long time, isn't it?

S: A few weeks.

Edelweiss: Speaking of deserts, I saw some campers, a couple with two children, put up a tent on the edge of one and retire for the night. Their experience in the desert cost them. During the night they were visited by a big rat which took a fancy to some of their jewelry, a pen, some spoons, and several bright stones the children had gathered, and made off with the lot, taking one item at a time while they slept.

S: You must mean a pack rat.

Edelweiss: It left something in "trade" for each item it stole, including some pebbles, a few seeds, and a piece of cactus with its needles still intact. The father rolled over during the night and wasn't too happy about the surprise he got from one of the rat's "presents."

S: What about the Grand Canyon, Edelweiss?

Edelweiss: Wonderful! I got into a small airplane with several tourists and we flew—or bumped—through the canyon and over the rough waters of the Colorado River as the guide/pilot explained the formations and their origins.

S: Edelweiss, did you sense the presence of any Native American spirits?

Edelweiss: In the canyon our pilot showed us some ancient adobe ruins, abandoned hundreds of years ago. I felt no spirit dwellers there. No bones have ever been found at the site, indicating that the dwellers left the area of their own accord, rather than having been slaughtered or driven out. Some 200-300 natives live and farm peacefully in a remote section. Most of your Native Americans who have left the Earth are now in their "Happy Hunting Ground" in Spirit.

S: Have you visited there?

Edelweiss: Yes, their life there is beautiful and secure both for man and animals. They worship God, Who is actually their Great Spirit. There they will never be driven off their land.

S: The Indian spirit guides, as many on Earth are privileged to have, dwell there.

Edelweiss: These guides were very spiritual on Earth and have evolved even higher in Spirit. They are peaceful.

S: And from the deserts and canyons?

Edelweiss: Continuing on my "Americanization" tour, I flew over one of the Seven Wonders of the Modern World, your Golden Gate Bridge. I'm glad in Spirit we don't have to construct these wonders. Whew!

S: In San Francisco, did you ride on one of those streetcars that go up and down the hills on cables, almost vertically?

Edelweiss: They are fun, but so crowded! If I had wings they would have been ruined, as I hung precariously out the door in a driving rain!

The people accept this crush as perfectly normal and dangle happily out windows and doors to get to their destinations, rain or shine!

S: There is a gay colony in San Francisco. What are your impressions?

Edelweiss: Native Americans held homosexuals to be spiritually blessed and honored them. There were no problems. Nobody called them names.

S: They are loyal friends, good citizens, and twice as sensitive as most male and female heterosexuals, having a deeper understanding and feeling for both their male and female friends. I wish I had this talent. I have never understood men. For that matter, I don't understand many women. But let's get on with your *Tour d'Amerique*.

Edelweiss: Did you know I'm a good skier?

S: I don't doubt it. Keep on.

Edelweiss: Especially when I'm hanging on behind while someone else does the skiing.

S: Where did you get your piggy-back ride?

Edelweiss: Aspen. The Rocky Mountains are breathtaking, literally. I wish I could have skied alone.

S: I have a picture of skis making tracks down the mountainside with no one on them.

Edelweiss: My orders from the Seraphim: Rule #1—no freaking out the natives.

S: Texas?

Edelweiss: I was saddened by the problem of illegal aliens crossing the border from México. They take a great risk in attempting to get in to the U.S., in order to get employment, education for their children, and in general a better life, with plenty to eat on the table. I am praying that one day México will provide for their poor and uneducated, with some kind of program of training and assistance. Sadly, I don't think it will be soon.

S: I will pray with you. I've seen many of these people seeking help where I work. They are bright and willing to work and go to school.

Edelweiss: I visited your colorful New Orleans.

S: Did you see any voodoo practices?

Edelweiss: In these times I think voodoo mostly is past history, in the cities anyway, where you will find tourist shops, but don't count out what may go on in the bayous away from the public eye. What I really enjoyed were the jazz musicians! These people are real. I saw a jazz funeral. The musicians marched ahead, followed by a fancy white and gold coach carrying the deceased, drawn by beautiful white horses with plumed headdress. Behind it walked the bereaved family and friends. These people really express their feelings. This is very healthy. They will miss their dear one but know he or she will have a beautiful life in the Spirit world. I was so touched. What a wonderful sendoff!

Florida was fun. At Marineland near St. Augustine some very interesting things were going on in the porpoise tank. I understand that since then they have separated the males and females. Your beaches are great. Wish I had a swim suit! Do you think I'd look good in a bikini? I loved Miami's Little Havana. I almost wished I could drink some of the heavenly smelling coffee! There are disadvantages in being an angel on Earth.

S: I know how you feel. I can't make coffee like that even when I use a brew labeled "Cuban coffee." Did you understand the language? Cubans like their colorful words and phrases.

Edelweiss: I learned those from *you*.

S: And I learned them from the Cubans. I hope you saw my old home town, Tampa, when the old neighborhoods, downtown shopping area, and dime stores were swinging. Ybor City, our Latin Quarter, with its many Spanish restaurants, cigar factories, Spanish import stores, and festivals, had real *alma* (soul). There will never be another place like it. Edelweiss, you left something out: Vegas.

Edelweiss: There are rules against children and angels gambling in the casinos. I would've loved to see a show, but wasn't permitted. (They probably feared I would see some male dancers in scant attire. Ridiculous!)

My experiences were all in all delightful, except for a few unpleasantries in some darker areas of the larger cities. I won't go into that, but the Seraphim wanted me to see the other side of life on Earth. I had to get the whole picture.

S: I'm glad you came, Edelweiss, and that you are one of my beloved angels. Interesting the way things work out.

Edelweiss: And not coincidentally.

S: In the next presidential election, I will vote for you. Edelweiss for president, on the Angel ticket.

Edelweiss: My campaign slogan will be, "A roller coaster in every town, and an angel in every home."

S: Make that five angels, and you're elected.

Edelweiss: Right on!

◆   ◆   ◆

September 29, 2000.

S: My angels, I am going to Canada next month to visit Rosie on her birthday. I know the neighbors will take care of Zora, but I will worry about her thinking I have deserted her.

Snowflake: No way. She will wait for you to return, as she always does.

S: She "talks" to me every time she comes in, telling me all about her great adventures outside chasing snakes, squirrels and lizards.

Snowflake: Go and have a good time. Don't worry. We're all watching out.

S: Thank God for you (and the Seraphim). Now may I speak to the most handsome, lovable, supremely talented and charming spirit of all?

Richard: You rang?

S: Richard, we have to do something about Pestiferous.

Richard: He had better be on good behavior.

S: He isn't. Two nights ago I head a thunderous noise from under the bed all the way through my pillow. Like a loud belch.

Richard: What did you have to eat before you went to bed?

S: Richard, *really*. It wasn't me. It was the spook. This morning he and Zora were romping under the dining room table in a big wrestling and punching bout.

Richard: Who won?

S: I'm glad they're friends, or else they would kill each other.

Richard: He's in the doghouse.

S: Why can animals see spirits when humans can't?

Richard: Because animals are very sensitive and haven't been taught to disbelieve in the metaphysical nor to fear spirit manifestations. There are some humans on Earth who can see spirits, but those are few.

S: I don't want to see them. I would absolutely freak out!

Richard: That's why you can't see them.

◆   ◆   ◆

October 24, 2000.

Edelweiss: You got home safely, just as we told you, and found everything just fine.

S: Thanks for everything. I had a wonderful time with Rosie and Roger in Mt. Elgin. Canada is beautiful this time of year, with trees resplendent in brilliant shades of red, gold and orange. I love Canada and her friendly people. We went up into the Mennonite community where people still use horse and buggy. You can tell which farms are Mennonite as there are no electric wires to the houses from the main highway cables. They still disdain luxuries of modern living. Married men have beards, the bachelors being clean shaven. We had lunch at a little restaurant where the waitress spoke to us with "thee" and "thou" pronouns. It was a wonderful trip, topped off by dinner with Roger's family. When I arrived home last night, I got a concert of high-pitched melodious meows, as though I had never been gone. If Zora could talk I'm sure I would hear about the wonderful care she got from her angels, neighbors and Pestiferous. I have a feeling that you are closer to her—and me—physically than you let on. She knows all of you, as I do. I wish all animals could have the care mine has, and all humans my blessings. When were the angels created?

Edelweiss: God created us long before man. Most of us are guardians.

S: Did God give you your names? Tell the people.

Rainbow: Every one of us has a name. If asked, your angels will tell you how many they are and give you their names, which will either be of nature (as we are called), happy, positive emotions, or religious fervor. Keep in close contact with them by telepathy or writing—whatever suits you best—and you will be amazed at what they can do for you. By their names you will know your angels, because those are words of things you love best or need most in your life. I will not give you examples. You will know them then you are told.

S: When Rosie was previously married, she drove with her husband on New Year's Eve to Tarpon Springs, a west coast Greek settlement, for lunch. On their way home, they stopped at an intersection for a light. A little lady Rosie described as "small and sweet-faced" with red, curly hair looked in the car window and asked for a ride. She got in the back seat, and as they were under way she put her hand on George's shoulder and said, "You are blessed and will soon live in a beautiful new home." As they approached a corner of a vacant lot, she said, "I'll get out here." On the curbing she thanked them and blessed both of them. They leaned out to say goodbye, and she had disappeared! The next day, George died in an accident. Rosie remembered the funny little red-haired lady. I said, "She was an angel."

Rosebud: A messenger angel. These are sent to foretell and to comfort. Her words made it easier for Rosie to accept the trauma of losing a loved one, knowing George would be happy in Spirit.

Edelweiss: There are things meant to happen, and only God knows why. These good people whose lives end tragically are more than compensated and will dwell in eternal glory. As much as you will miss their physical presence, be comforted knowing this. Call on your angels. They will help you to communicate with your loved ones in Spirit. Remember these good souls will miss you as much as you miss them. If you need earthly help, however, be careful with whom you seek spiritual assistance. Use your angels or a trusted minister, or both. Spiritual help is always available.

◆   ◆   ◆

November 6, 2000.

S: Rosie called today. She lost her beloved little West Highland Terrier, Abigail.

Edelweiss: We know. Snowflake, Dewdrop and Rosebud have been with her, and told us right away when she drew her last little breath. We're so sorry.

S: Abby was blind and ill. Though sad, it's really a blessing. Will you take care of her?

Edelweiss: You know we will.

Snowflake: We have her. She is still sleeping. When she awakens, she will soon be happy, and very healthy, with us; A bit disoriented at first, but we will make her feel loved and at home very soon. She will recognize Mike. She liked him.

S: Bless all of you. I know you will spoil her. Will she have her own little bed?

Snowflake: We still have Mike's bed that he disdained for lap service. It will fit her fine, unless *she* also insists on laps, which is very possible!

S: Richard, there is much excitement in the good old U.S. of A. We're having an election tomorrow for president. I hope our new one will be a good leader.

Richard: There is a big surprise in store.

S: What do you mean?

Richard: You will see.

S: It will be along night counting the votes from all over the country.

Richard: Longer than you think.

S: Anyway, thanks for looking after Abigail. Tell her we miss her.

Richard: We will. Good night. Love you.

S: Good night, love.

◆   ◆   ◆

November 16, 2000.

S: We had a nice rain! The plants and I are re-charged and we had a harmless hurricane season here, thanks to Dewdrop and Rainbow. We need more rain, though, hint, hint. How is Abby?

Snowflake: She is fine and frisky, in perfect health, with clear, sharp eyes. She knows where she is and is adapting beautifully.

S: Wait until I tell you about Abby's memorial service.

Snowflake: Wonderful!

S: Rosie was in such a state from losing her that the local vicar, Reverend Jane, held a service for Abby at Rosie's home, with candles burning brightly and Scottish bagpipe music in the background. Roger and his son Kyle and some friends and neighbors attended. It really helped Rosie to deal with losing her 13-year-old baby. Abby's ashes are in a beautiful urn in a special place in the house. I wonder how Rosie found bagpipe music.

Edelweiss: Dewdrop and Rosebud zeroed in on a music store and put a bug in Rosie's ear.

S: Are Abigail and Mike friends?

Snowflake: Yes. At first Jericho was a little jealous but is now joining in the romps. They get a little rambunctious at times, but its okay so long as they don't knock down the plants.

◆   ◆   ◆

December, 2000.

S: Richard, another year is coming to an end!

Richard: It's time for an evaluation of your progress during the year 2000.

S: Oh-oh. Did we do this last year?

Richard: No, but we should talk about it from now on.

S: You always fuss at me, what's the big deal just now?

Richard: Maybe the rating of A, B or F should be employed.

S: What happened to C and D?

Richard: If you go under B, spiritually, you might as well get an F.

S: Can't we just use "satisfactory?" I might sleep better.

Richard: *You* worry about sleep? You sleep like a log.

S: My clear conscience. Okay—shoot.

Richard: I will not shoot you, even though I am tempted to do so at times.

Edelweiss: She means "proceed."

Richard: I know.

S: Edelweiss is on my side.

Richard: She is laughing. She and the other angels know I do right by you.

S: You are my greatest friends, next to Jesus.

Richard: He expects me to guide and influence you effectually. If I fail, I will join Jericho in the doghouse.

S: Big kiss.

Richard: That's better. Now: your attitude, generosity, and contact with us are above reproach. I've worried some in the past over your resentment of those both on Earth and in Spirit who have hurt or offended you. I think now you have finally found the right path concerning grudges.

S: About those on Earth who are insensitive and envious, those who take me for granted and have been good to me only condescendingly, and those who have been downright offensive, I have decided it was done because they felt I am better than they are and are therefore defensive toward me.

Richard: They know exactly how you feel, you can be sure.

S: Therefore, I feel sorry for them and leave them to God's devices. They don't exist as far as I am concerned.

About those who have left the Earth, I will confess my relating to the musical, "Scrooge," in which one of Scrooge's debtors dances on his coffin singing, "Thank you very much!" I've decided that all the garbage I've taken should be dissolved by the wonderful gift those dear, departed ones have bestowed on me and all mankind, and I forgive them, not for their sake, but for mine. I am liberated, they are not. How does that sound to you?

Richard: Good—so long as you don't dance on their coffins.

S: Temptation conquered.

Richard: The truth has set you free. And don't forget to hold your tongue when you drop something on your foot, get impatient in traffic, or are entertained in the middle of the night by your enthusiastic little spirit.

S: Who belches loudly in the middle of the night!

Richard: Cussing won't help. All in all, I'd say you have ended year 2000 in a brighter note.

S: I love you and the angels more than ever, if that means anything.

Richard: It does, my brave little "pupil." We also love you.

S: Good night, love.

Richard: May all your dreams be sweet and fulfilled.

◆　　　◆　　　◆

2001!!
January.

S: My angels.

Edelweiss: Where have you been so far this year?

S: Fighting with house insurance, car insurance, drought, Pestiferous, drought, income tax returns, drought, Pestiferous...

Edelweiss: We get the drift. Everything will work out fine.

S: Did I mention drought?

Edelweiss: Several times.

S: I am fossilized.

Edelweiss: You are always turning into a fossil. Have you checked the weather report today?

S: *Possible* rain. Maybe you angels could perform what our ancient Native Americans did so effectively—a rain dance. It worked every time. Who is the best dancer among you?

Rosebud: Rainbow. She dances around between the clouds on a rainy day and colorfully lights up the sky.

Snowflake: Just like you to think of something romantic, Rosebud!

Dewdrop: I'll do that rain dance! (Rainbow will give me a few pointers.) Remember, I start the rain, she ends it.

S: That should do it. I'm going to tell Richard about Pestiferous. This one is a guillotine offense, with drums rolling.

Richard: I know, he confessed. But tell me.

S: Last night I was reading in bed when I heard a loud sound in the dining room. I ran in and found the door to the back yard wide open. No damage, but the handle lock was still set. I knew immediately what had happened.

Richard: He kicked the door open.

S: This is the worst yet. Not only did it scare Zora and me, but the door was wide open and available to any intruder that might be around.

Richard: Actually, the door, although you had locked it, was not closed securely, and anyone could have opened it easily. He banged the door out making so you would investigate. He didn't know how else to handle the situation.

S: Then he was really trying to protect us! I remember pulling the door securely afterwards.

Richard: He frightened you and Zora. I'm sorry.

S: Just the same, I appreciate what he did. It will remind me to be more careful.

◆   ◆   ◆

The Children: Winners!

S: Rainbow, tell me about the children in Spirit.

Rainbow: Ideally, children are born safely on Earth to caring, loving parents, and raised in a happy, secure home. Some, however, do not survive on Earth: stillborns, babies, tots, young children, teenagers. They will all grow up in Spirit until they reach the age of 33, when through their learning processes they can become spirit guides or serve in other spiritual vocations.

S: What about aborted unborns?

Rainbow: The decision is made upon their arrival whether they are to reincarnate or be received as newborns. The angels are very wary about returning them to Earth unless they were miscarried by loving parents-to-be who grieved at their loss.

S: Are these the only reincarnations?

Rainbow: There are many others, but that is a matter of past-life Karma to be resolved and handled by the angels. This is a well-planned and well-programmed procedure. Sometimes an enlightened spirit will request rebirth on the Earth plane to fulfill a desired vocation or a special destination in life not acquired in a previous life.

S: How, where, and by whom are the children received?

Rainbow: They are welcomed into a special haven or nursery called "The Garden of Loving Arms." The babies and other small ones are attended by loving angel "nannies" or nurses until they are ready to be placed.

S: Placed?

Rainbow: As we told you, there are many different Spirit communities, with many prospective parents and families anxious to make the new arrivals their own. The older children are attended lovingly for an adjustment period by angels who gently explain what has happened to them, and what their lives will be here.

S: The must miss their families on Earth terribly.

Rainbow: Some are glad to be away from them. Others are distraught, and they are consoled with the promise of being united with the Earth families some day. Children adjust well; that is one of the advantages of childhood. I know how sad their Earth families are to lose them, but please tell them their little ones are well cared for and living in a perfect atmosphere of love and well being. Remember them happily and thank God for their deliverance. They will reunite one day. That is God's promise.

S: How are they raised?

Rainbow: The children are carefully observed for special talents and preferences. Some show interest in sciences, others the arts or other professions. According to their interests, they are placed in loving families in the proper community or garden. The children are delighted and happily anticipate the future.

Children grow up in Spirit much as they do on Earth. They attend school, have duties to perform, attend services, and even have parties! Their social life is very important. Spirit children are gregarious and fun-loving. They have a happy and harmonious life.

Children here are much respected and show respect to all in return. They are taught independence and are encouraged to pursue their own interests. Besides spiritual enhancement, they paint, sing, dance, write poetry and essays, help with the younger children, tend animals and gardens, and above all, join in our praise and celebration of God, Who is greatly pleased with them.

S: The so-called "Wild ones," young adults or teenagers whose rebellious attitude here on Earth has led them to drugs, sex, and other destructive activities?

Richard: These are easier to deal with here, as they are in awe of their new world. They enjoy their teachings here for the realization of what love and respect bring to their lives. Their activities here, including sports, school, assigned duties and interaction with others of all ages have contributed to their self-image most positively.

Edelweiss: In a word, "cool."

S: Everything seems to be based on common sense and morality.

Richard: Two of our greatest gifts both here and on Earth. Without both, nothing functions satisfactorily. One needs the other. When a child learns to love himself and others, has respect for all God's creatures and environment, a sense of humor, and a positive attitude overall, what do we have? *A winner!*

S: You have told me that those in Spirit are gathered together by their professions and interests. What about the ministers of all denominations?

S: Sadly, there are those who are spending some time in the reconciliation process. They did not resist the temptation to take advantage of people's trust to gain materially and otherwise. They are ashamed, and if ever allowed to minister again they must atone completely. You'd be surprised, some of these "reformed" pastors make great spirit guides. They latch on to Earth ministers who might be tempted and steer them accordingly. Those ministers with whom God is pleased may choose a vocation in Spirit as spirit guides, teachers, and helping the angels in welcoming and counseling new arrivals, both children and adults. They may be allowed rebirth to continue the spiritual work on Earth to which they were dedicated.

S: Scientists?

Richard: There is much concern about endangerment of plants and animals, and about contamination. We have spirit working hard with your courageous animal activists and environmentalists. Certain harmful chemicals that poison the soil and waters have been outlawed, along with fishing regulations that save thousands of dolphins.

S: I feel very strongly in favor of these laws, but I hate sharks and alligators. What good do they do except maim and kill people and animals?

Richard: There is a reason for everything. Perhaps one day important drugs or some other scientific discovery will justify God's placement on Earth of these seemingly out of place species. The old cliché—God works in strange ways—may be the answer. I talked to a scientist in the Garden of the Future, which also includes inventors, doctors, and architects, about global warming. He wants all chemicals which can be absorbed into the atmosphere, such as your hair spray, Sarah, banned.

S: There you go about my hair spray.

Richard: When you were young, you did beautifully without it. You didn't need it then, and you don't need it now. The government is loath to displease voters in banning some products.

S: They have enough to worry about!

Richard: One very small factor among thousands contaminating land and atmosphere.

S: You're going to have farmers, utility companies, fishermen and politicians kicking my butt.

Richard: Only some, especially the politicians. It's a big concern to us in Spirit who loved and still love beautiful Earth.

S: Just one more: what happens to the undertakers?

Richard: They never again want to see a dead body, and never will. They happily pursue other interests.

S: People will be surprised at the great organization and activity of your world!

Richard: We're a busy place. No harps played around here. You will be put to work, most pleasantly.

S: No housework, cooking or raking leaves! Whee! But I'll miss my hair spray.

Richard: You know you won't. Your hair will look exactly the way you want it without the spray.

S: I know! What about clothes?

Richard: You will wear the soft, comfortable and beautiful clothes in the style all the ladies here wear, and can choose the colors you want.

S: I think I'm going to like it there!

Richard: I know you will.

◆   ◆   ◆

February 11, 2001. Jericho.

S: Richard: I hope your guillotine is sharpened and polished for a special occasion.

Richard: I know.

S: Twice lately, I've seen something that looks like the behind of a small, white animal scooting around a door or under the desk in my room.

Richard: This is one of your Pestiferous' cute tricks.

S: It's bad enough to *hear* him, worse to see the bandit. Especially his behind!

Richard: I have absolutely forbidden him to materialize again—ever—in any shape, size or form. He really means no harm. Please don't worry. It will not happen again.

S: Does he look like that, really? A small animal?

Richard: He can take on different appearances even though he has his own natural look.

S: Spare me. But don't go away—you haven't heard it all. Last night, I turned over and he yelled loudly, as though I hurt him rolling over on him.

Richard: You can't hurt him. He can flatten himself as thin as a sheet of paper.

S: I know, because Zora paws under afghans and rugs chasing him.

Richard: I'm sorry. He's just having fun.

S: It sounded like "Owww!"

Richard: He's in the doghouse.

S: He thinks he's Mr. Funny Man.

Richard: Just be glad he has a sense of humor instead of evil intentions. He is crying because we won't let him play with his best friends.

S: What do Mike and Abigail do when he's in trouble?

Richard: They ask if he can play, and I say no. I even threatened to get them another playmate if he doesn't behave.

S: That's mean.

Richard: No meaner than you cussing him out and telling him to go to hell. At least my methods work—for a while, anyway.

S: I'm glad I have you.

Richard: Are you really?

S: I love you.

Richard: And I you. Please be patient with Jericho.

◆　　　◆　　　◆

February 15, 2001.

S: Richard, how do you like our manuscript so far?

Richard: It needs a little more "pizzazz." (I learned that word from some American theater people.)

S: Did you like them?

Richard: Very much. They were fun to work with.

S: Do you like our modern artists?

Richard: You have many fine singers, and their performances are available to us. Your opera and classical music are wonderful.

S: How do you see them? Do you have TVs?

Richard: Sometimes we watch programs that appear as though projected on a wall here. For the most part Dewdrop and Rosebud use this medium for their information, along with others.

Rosebud: Edelweiss watches "As the World Turns."

Edelweiss: It comes on by surprise when I'm looking for other events.

S: And "pop" music?

Richard: Very entertaining, but I would enjoy the young female singers more if they would cover up more.

S: When I was young, the dress for which I received the most compliments was a long-sleeved, high-neckline white dress with a sparkling belt buckle. It didn't hide my good figure at all.

Richard: Men are not stupid. They know what's underneath. They don't have to have it thrown at them.

S: Do you have favorite pop artists?

Richard: I like Barbra Streisand and Elton John. They are very entertaining and classy!

S: *Sir* Elton, please! Her Majesty knighted him recently.

Richard: I'm not surprised.

S: You mentioned "pizzazz." Does that mean spicy? You want to present an "X-rated" manuscript to publishers?

Richard: It's very decent.

S: I have a story to tell, if it doesn't gross anyone out.

Richard: I'm all ears.

S: Some time ago, I had some work done on my septic tank, and a big load of dirt was brought in to cover the drain field. Soon after a rain, I saw a large bone in that area. I studied it and convinced myself it was an animal bone. The workmen returned a few days later to finish their work, and when they left the bone as missing.

Richard: It was a human leg bone.

S: Where did it come from? I hope not an ancient burial ground.

Richard: No, those are protected. A man, while out hunting, died on that spot where the dirt was dug up, over 100 years ago. He was never found.

S: Poor man. What happened to the bone in my yard?

Richard: When the workmen saw it, they took it away and buried it elsewhere. The "mystery man" is all right in Spirit, and is not upset about his bone. Say a prayer and bless the ground where it lay. Then forget it.

◆　　　◆　　　◆

March, 2001.

S: A cedar tree next door, rare because pencil factories have all but obliterated cedars in Florida, has died from the drought. I'm going to propose a law changing the name of Cedar Key, Florida, to "Pencil Key."

Richard: Oh-oh. Sounds like Grouch Day.

S: I'm always grouchy, mostly from lack of sleep. Pestiferous kept me awake night before last tapping musically on my cranberry glass collection on my bedroom wall shelf.

Richard: He told me what you called him.

S: And last night I was awakened by a sound coming up; through my pillow, a tooting, buzzy sound like a kazoo.

Snowflake: Should I ask what a kazoo is?

Rosebud: Edelweiss, do you know?

Rainbow: I do. It comes in different colors, and—

Dewdrop: Mine is black.

Edelweiss: It's a child's toy tooter. They gave them to children at parties to drive the adults nuts.

Snowflake: Oh, the kids love them.

S: Would someone please take Pestiferous' away from him so I can rest without his jazz performance?

Richard: He told me about the glass and kazoo performances.

S: I have to admit he has perfect rhythm. Did he learn his musicality from you?

Richard: Don't forget all those recordings you have, and the TV programs of music. He listens to it all.

S: He's quiet today. What did you do?

Richard: You will notice Zora is not playing with him.

S: She seems to look at something, then shakes her head and runs away.

Richard: It's an old spirit trick. To her, he smells terrible.

S: Richard! Even for *him*, that's mean.

Richard: He cried and said I'm taking all his best friends away. Animals here are all running off at great speed. I told him if he behaved himself he wouldn't lose any friends.

S: Just when I think he's exhausted all his schemes he comes up with something else unique. I'm steeling myself for his next performance. But, I'm almost sorry for him. He's so clean, and you make him stink to Zora!

Richard: It worked. One has to be merciless with Jericho.

◆   ◆   ◆

March 14, 2001.

S: I took Zora to the vet today. She behaved very well but there was a big shepherd next to us in the waiting room having nervous fits.

Snowflake: Richard was laughing about that. Here he is.

Richard: Did you forget you gave Jericho permission to go with you to the vet?

S: He was so quiet I didn't know he was with us!

Richard: He got in the car with you and into the clinic.

S: Why were you laughing?

Richard: That big dog you mentioned. Jericho was right in front of her, glaring.

S: Her owner said she had never seen her act that way. The cocker spaniel on her lap growled. I've never in my life been growled at by an animal!

Richard: Every minute you were near those dogs Jericho was watching like a hawk to ensure that Zora, even in her carrier, was safe. He wouldn't do anything mean to the dogs, but you can be sure that nothing will ever occur to Zora similar to what happened to Mike. He knows how to intimidate them.

S: What does he do?

Richard: I told you he can take on any form. This time he was a big hairy monster with great green fangs snarling at them.

S: That poor big dog. She was a real sweetie and wouldn't hurt a fly. Maybe I shouldn't let him go along with us.

Richard: No, he's very grateful to go. He adores Zora and means to protect her!

S: My cat has a spook bodyguard!

Richard: You had better believe it. Don't worry. He's not going to do anything violent unless Zora is attacked.

S: What if dogs, or even humans, try to hurt her?

Richard: Don't ask.

S: I'm asking.

Richard: There would be dogs and people flying in all directions. I told you of his potential strength. He won't use it unless he is terrified for her. Or *you.*

S: Please tell him to go easier on his victims. Convince him also *not* to materialize!

Richard: That is a promise.

S: Or to steal any more of my craft supplies. I had six beads to use in a necklace on the spare bedroom dresser. One morning I noticed two beads were missing. I told him I'd better find the missing beads in their box the next day. I checked the next morning and all six were there. I will not tolerate crooked spooks in my house.

Richard: You didn't tell me about that one.

S: Well, he made it good so I let it go.

◆   ◆   ◆

March 22,2001.

S: My angels?

Edelweiss: Our Sarah, what's up?

S: Just wanted to chat.

Rosebud: Richard loves the flowers you put by his picture.

S: Just simple wild flowers.

Rosebud: The best kind. Most important is that they are from you.

S: I also put some at my brother Morris' "shrine." I wonder if he knows.

Snowflake: Whatever you do for someone in Spirit, be it flowers, prayers, or just a loving thought, believe that it is known and appreciated. Your loved ones here are well aware of your loyalty and fond remembrance, which will be repaid a thousand times.

S: He was always so good to me. I felt he was the only one in my family that really loved me.

Dewdrop: And, like you, was never a bigot.

S: At a wedding in which he was an usher, none of the others wanted to seat a lovely, dark East Indian lady, and Morris seated her so quickly she never even noticed.

Dewdrop: Don't think we weren't aware of that!

S: One of the proudest moments of my life was when one of my grown daughters told me, "Mom, in our life together, there was never an ethnic slur uttered in our house." I never even thought of it until she mentioned it. Both my girls are broadminded and sensitive, thank

God. Maybe Morris' long military career was instrumental in forming his attitudes.

Rainbow: You were both born that way.

Edelweiss: We'd better shove off now. Someone is shifting impatiently.

S: Do I hear mooing?

Richard: Loudly. Hello, my little sparrow.

S: That's a new one. You never called me that before.

Richard: You remind me of a small bird, flying freely and wanting freedom for others. No one will ever cage you. You are what your people call a "free spirit." You will stay only where you want to be, not by force.

S: I guess you know me pretty well.

Richard: I ought to, and I do.

S: Do I sense that you are gong to fuss at me?

Richard: Do I sense a guilt feeling?

S: You heard what I said today.

Richard: I did indeed.

S: Big hug.

Richard: That's better.

S: And a big kiss.

Richard: Better still. How is your friend Pestiferous behaving?

S: The other night as I was going to sleep I heard a soft "hm." A few seconds later another "hm." Then a long sigh.

Richard: Trying to get your attention.

S: As I write, I'm hearing a few taps.

Richard: He knows when we are in contact.

S: Don't tell him I said so, but in spite of myself I'm beginning to like the little bandit. I'm getting sleepy. Tell me something nice.

Richard: I always tell you nice things.

S: Give me three.

Richard: 1: I love you. 2: I want to spend eternity with you. 3: You still cuss.

S: You had to ruin it.

Richard: You tell me three things.

S: 1: I love you. 2: My greatest wish is to be with you in the Garden of Song. 3: I'm sorry I cussed. I hear Pestiferous. Did you punish him for "humming" at me?

Richard: Only a lecture. You weren't that upset.

S: Thanks for being with me a while tonight. Good night, my sexy phantom.

Richard: Good night, my own.

◆   ◆   ◆

April 15, 2001.

S: Happy Easter! God bless all of you. I know you had a glorious day in the garden, with beauty all around you and the Presence of Our Lord.

Edelweiss: We did something different this time. Rainbow planned activities for the children—painting, weaving, singing, games, and of course prayer. Jesus was fascinated and wanted the whole day's activities to be centered around the young ones. He sat by the Fountain of Life and watched their antics, laughing delightedly at their fun and joy. It was a most charming and heart-warming time, and all of us, including Jesus, couldn't have had a more rewarding day.

S: What did they paint, Rainbow?

Rainbow: They wanted to paint Jesus! When their art work was done, he remarked that he didn't know he was that handsome! Then they insisted he paint something. It was a dove in flight. For an amateur, as he called himself, it was very good. The children propped it in the branches of a tree near the Fountain for all to see.

"The Dove of the Holy Spirit is perching in our tree!" exclaimed one child.

"Every time you see the dove," said Jesus, "remember that He dwells in our hearts. Feel His presence and all the beauty of the Earth and Spirit will be yours."

S: Tell me about the Easter gifts for the children.

Rainbow: Each child was given a pet of his or her own choice. Jesus laughed at the reaction as each child received a rabbit, dog, cat, guinea pig and so on, even a baby goat! The children surprised Jesus with a beautiful red hen. He had it in his arms when he left.

S: Jesus has a *chicken* for a pet?

Snowflake: He named her Rebeccah. He thinks she's great.

S: Why, he is just like one of the children!

Rainbow: Just pray that we never lose the child within us. When we do, we lose our ability to learn, to trust, to love, to believe, to anticipate all beauty in our lives. The child within us will never let us down. It will always be a part of our happiness on Earth and in Spirit.

S: Thank you for sharing your beautiful day with me.

◆　　　◆　　　◆

April 4, 2001.

Edelweiss: You are sad. Rosebud said you found Clarissa.

S: While out walking this evening, I saw a big black snake on the side of the road.

Snowflake: It was Clarissa. She was trying to get across the road and was run over by a car. Grieve no more. St. Francis has a nice rock garden with plenty of foliage for her. She's happy.

S: Thank God for him. These next two weeks I will be involved in kitty-sitting for Noel several evenings, as she will be in Cuba attending a faculty development seminar at the University of Havana.

Dewdrop: Being around animals is good for you.

S: While taking my walks in the evenings I usually stop to pet some friends of mine along the way. Several dogs in the neighborhood wait for me by their fences to say hello. One big rottweiler, not yet grown, is so big already he gently takes my whole hand in his mouth up to the wrist. (I'm glad he likes me!) Whenever I've been around other animals, Zora sniffs me accusingly.

Snowflake: She's jealous. She thinks you are exclusively hers.

Rosebud: Richard is here.

Richard: Sorry about Clarissa. She's happy here.

S: Sometimes I wish I were with all of you just for a while, so I could rest my head on your shoulders.

Richard: You can so that spiritually, for now, and one day in person.

S: At least Pestiferous is being very good.

Richard: He told me you had complimented him on taking such good care of Zora, and that you told her he loved her. He is very proud of himself. He will get a big head.

S: I am happy for his protection but I don't want to see any white rumps—or any other part of him.

Richard: He'd better obey me.

S: I received a new tape of your movie "Land of Smiles," improved in sound and picture over the old one I had. I love it. Those American ladies were right, you *do* look like a teddy bear!

Richard: Oh? Why?

S: You know why. They are chubby and cuddly.

Richard: I'm blushing.

S: Right. Like I'm turning blue.

Richard: The only thing blue is the air around you at some times.

S: Herr Comedian. The flowers I put by your picture lasted a long time. I'll get some fresh ones.

Richard: Nothing will ever last as long as my love.

S: Nor mine. Richard, do you remember what you called me the other night?

Richard: Let's see. Was it Garbage Mouth?

S: No.

Richard: The Purple Fog?

S: No. You called me your wife. Do you want a divorce?

Richard: Don't joke about it! I have no intention of ever giving you up. You have the possibility of being a really evolved spirit some day, and we will work together happily ever after. But there is much work to be done

S: Yeah, there are still some kinks in the old machine yet, and things to accomplish, like—right now—our story.

Richard: You've come a long way; that's very encouraging. Don't let hate come back into your life.

S: There is no one worth my tendering them that much negative energy! I don't love many people in a personal way, but I don't wish anyone harm. You and the angels have helped me so much. Tell me, in the garden will we have our own little home?

Richard: Yes, and many pets.

S: And children?

Richard: Well, you won't bear them, but there are plenty to go around of all ages and races. Beautiful children, all of them.

S: We will raise some of the children. I hope they will be guides some day.

Richard: Remember, they must choose for themselves.

S: Yes, as on Earth, they must think for themselves. With our guidance, of course!

Richard: Since you love children so much, they are bound to be happy and motivated!

◆　　　◆　　　◆

April 15, 2001.

S: Richard, don't tell me I've been watching too many fantasy movies, but in Spirit can we travel back in time on Earth and witness events in past history?

Richard: What particular event or events would interest you?

S: For one, ancient Rome and Greece. Only I might be afraid of being thrown to the lions in the Colisseum.

Richard: Guides and angels have been granted this, but only in, you might call it, "researching" events of those times, experiencing what occurred and why the leaders and people acted and reacted thus. Terrifying, at times, and extremely interesting. Spirits know Earth history, but it is more fascinating and realistic to actually "live" a while in those times and learn to understand the people, their problems, their customs, language, accomplishments, and, of course, failures. Many questions are answered. And to answer your *next* one, I haven't made any ventures yet. I hope to feel the Earth under my feet again, talk to the people, and visit some of my old "haunts." The world has changed so much. I would like to start back when I was performing, and then visit in eras, study the changes in the arts, customs, character through the years. I would attend, if possible, performances of many of the "greats" such as Caruso and Gigli.

S: And Richard Tauber?

Richard: I wouldn't mind watching the old boy sing again on stage.

S. Meaning you! I hope to be with you then.

Richard: An excellent thought.

S: Just thinking of it gives me goose pimples.

Richard: I'm glad I know what that means, or I might think you caught something from a goose.

S: Would you reappear on Earth as Richard Tauber?

Richard: Heavens, no. I might scare myself to death. It will be more fun going incognito, just a tourist in town for the sights.

S: We'll hit the spots. I've still got "goosies" thinking about it.

Richard: And sleepy eyes, I think.

S: Good night, Love you *beaucoup*.

Richard: Good night, my one and only love.

◆   ◆   ◆

May 1, 2001.

S: Gasp!

Edelweiss: Oh-oh. The drought again.

Dewdrop: She's fossilizing. I can hear the cracking and crunching.

S: Very funny. You angels should be on the comedy writing team of a TV sitcom.

Rosebud: Don't let them tease you, Sarah. We know how badly you need rain.

Rainbow: You should get some this month. When bad winds come this summer, I'll be there.

S: Where's Snowflake?

Snowflake: Present, listening to the dumb fossil jokes.

S: I'm ignoring them. Have you named the new little residents yet? The mother dog what was killed on the highway, and her ten puppies that were drowned?

Snowflake: St. Francis is letting us have all of them! Annie is the mama, and her four boys are Mikie, Paddy, Andy and Ollie. The six girls are Maggie, Flossie, Franny, Bunny, Krissie and Sophie. Like their mother, they're small and tan short-hairs. All happy to be together.

S: I'd like to turn whoever neglected her and killed her darling babies over to Edelweiss. They would hear a few things in graphic elegance.

Edelweiss: And get a swift kick.

Rosebud: Richard is here.

Richard: I know about Jericho's performance last night.

S: Apparently he was trying to emulate a stunt pilot, whooshing noisily about the room just as I was about to go to sleep. He's not helping me in my quest for holier expression of my language arts. He's being very quiet, except for a tap or two. Zora was looking around for him tonight.

Richard: He is crying because we wouldn't let him play with his buddies for a while. They feel sorry for him and ask our forgiveness. We can't let him get away with too much. I told you about imps. They need strict disciplining. Don't worry. He wants to be a "good boy" and to be guided. He understands his punishments.

S: Richard, have you told Jesus about Jericho?

Richard: He laughed. He said you must be all right if an *imp* loves you and wants to protect you.

S: *And* Zora!

Richard: He was amazed.

S: He is so wonderful, so human and yet so godlike. So perfect and yet so understanding of our earthly foibles.

Richard: We can't be perfect, but we can show our gratitude for his blessings by trying to shed some of the Light he has given us to others.

S: I'm trying. I told you I would forgive.

Richard: But for *your* sake, you said. Do it for others' sake also.

S: I will not blither.

Richard: What is that?

S: I will bow and crawl on my knees only to Our Lord. I won't deliberately hurt anyone, but no one will break my spirit. That's been tried before.

Richard: That's not the point. You don't have to blither. (I take it that's another of your Americanism. I will look it up in the Records.)

S: Tell me about these Records.

Richard: I had to open my big mouth. You know Records are kept in Spirit. Everything that happens or has ever happened is recorded in detail. Every time you cuss it appears in the Records.

S: What?!

Richard: Really. You must get some Sleep now.

S: Sleep? I'm wide awake with big owl eyes. That's shameful. I don't think bad words should appear in Records kept in an innocent world.

Richard: Then don't say them.

S: Mr. Tough Guy, huh?

Richard: For my own sake, I'm glad I'm Mr. Tough Guy. As your guide, I'd jolly well best be tough!

S: Okay, Mr. Toughie. I love you and will sleep with you in my heart.

Richard: And I with you in mine. Good night, my one and only cusser.

S: Good night, my one and only Mr. Tough Guy.

◆　　　◆　　　◆

May 16, 2001.

S: Edelweiss, Rainbow, Dewdrop, Snowflake and Rosebud!

All: Good evening, and bless you and Richard.

S: Thank you, my angels. I want to wish Richard a happy birthday on his arrival on Earth. May he be blessed throughout eternity.

Angels: And you with him! Here he is.

Richard: I love the roses. Thank you.

S: I wish I could hand them to you, but for now the best I can do is place them by your picture near your music. I watched two of your movies tonight. I wanted to step into the screen and hug you.

Richard: Some day you won't have to step through a television set. You will be here with me.

S: Richard, I was thinking about your parents today while getting your flowers. You haven't talked much about them.

Richard: You will meet them.

S: I just wanted to know they are with you and happy.

Richard: Sublimely! We're all together. You have always been a happy person on Earth, and will be even more so here.

S: Will they like me?

Richard: Foolish question. They will love you dearly.

S: And I they. I don't deserve all my blessings.

Richard: Let God be the judge of that. He knows what's inside one's heart. Some people can fool themselves, but not God. They live in a dream world. Your feet are planted firmly on the ground, as the saying goes. You have no illusions about yourself. You are *you*, and that's that. And I love the you that you are!

S: You have a way with words.

Richard: Speaking of words...

S: I only said one today.

Richard: I counted two.

S: I'm sorry I swore on your birthday.

Richard: Forgiven. You really mean no harm, but it's ugly.

S: I will do penance. I won't even cuss at Jericho. I can hear his royal impness now, tapping around. I'm glad he's reformed, even though he performs a few shenanigans now and then. He and Zora are buddies. Sometimes, however, he appears to restrain her; she likes to play rough. She grabs my hand in her two front paws and gives me a staccato pounding with her hind legs. All of a sudden she will stop, look surprised, and jump off the bed. I think he scolds her for getting a bit rough.

Richard: He does scold her, but gently. He doesn't want her to fear him.

S: A while ago she jumped up on the wall about four feet, after him, I'm sure.

Richard: His favorite places are behind the TV, under the couch, in the bathtub behind the curtain, and under your bed.

S: He must know we're communicating, as he is tapping excitedly. Just don't let him materialize. I would absolutely *freak*.

Richard: He wont. He doesn't want another stink zap.

S: I wish I knew how you did that.

Richard: Professional secret.

S: Well, it worked. Let us all give thanks.

The Dawn Will Come

S: Richard, can you tell me about the future on Earth? At present we have so many problems.

Richard: And when didn't Earth have problems?

S: Not this many. War, crime, over-population, AIDS, environmental ruin and ecological imbalances, extinction of species, global warming, you name it!

Richard: There is much yet to accomplish, much work to be done, but eventually the New Dawn will cast its light and there will be a new movement on Earth, one of harmony and cooperation between nations.

S: The New Dawn?

Richard: The Dawn of Enlightenment. When men will be touched by the gentle and mighty Holy Spirit, and love and understanding will foster the greatest peace and harmony ever experienced on Earth.

Pray for your brave peacemakers who both on Earth and in Spirit strive to bring about world peace—our prayers will make them even stronger. We are part of it all.

S: When will this come?

Richard: Not so far off as one might think. There is one among you, a great leader not as of yet to the fore, who by his simplicity and sincerity and great common sense will impress and sway even the most impassioned dissenter and bring the world to a better place in which to live and thrive. His spirits are working hard with him now. Pray with them. People in the New Dawn will obey God not because they are afraid of Him, but only because they love Him, as a child will obey his parents because he trusts them and wants to please them, not because they might whale the daylights out of him. Common sense as well as morality will prevail. Sin and crime will be avoided, not just because they are wrong, but because they are stupid. If all of you on Earth totally understood our world here in our lovely gardens, I can truly tell you that not a single crime more would be committed there, so anxious would all be to get here! It is a complete world. A fun world, a blessed world filled with beauty, love and contentment. Jesus has said, "O ye of little faith." He summed up in five words that you cannot express in a million, in regard to your problems. *Think. Believe. Pray.*

I am but a small voice in the universe, but Sarah, I hope I have inspired a belief in yourself, faith in God, and actions generated by love and common sense. I am happy to be your guide, and delighted that you will be here with me some day. God bless and love you and all who may be inspired by my words. You have everything before you. It's your choice. As Edelweiss would say, "Don't blow it."

Epilogue

✤

No More Mr. Nice Guy!

September, 2001.

All of the preceding pages were finished many weeks before the September 11 devastating terrorist attack on the World Trade Center and Pentagon, and the crash in Pennsylvania, at which time I had been refinishing the manuscript. These unspeakable acts of cowardice, sadism and pure evil left all the decent world in horror, outrage and heartbreak.

As I recovered from shock, I decided I would be remiss in omitting the feelings I shared with my Spirit family. Needless to say, my very outspoken spirits vented their anger in the most graphic terms.

◆   ◆   ◆

September 11, 2001.

S: Oh, my God! We're at war!

Edelweiss: Let it be known on your beautiful Earth that the angels and all the good spirits are banded together as an army and will fight alongside your brave soldiers with all our power to end this war against the forces of evil behind these acts of terrorism.

S: And these forces of evil?

Rainbow: Your government knows exactly who they are, and in particular who their leader is.

109

Snowflake: He is brilliant, rich, and totally evil. A very lethal combination.

Dewdrop: He is having a good laugh, knowing all the damage and grief he has propagated.

Rosebud: He will choke on his laughter! Count on it.

S: Thank you for your comforting words, sweet angels. So much damage has been done, so many lives lost, so much heartbreak.

Edelweiss: We are sharing it with all of you on Earth who represent decency.

◆   ◆   ◆

September 14, 2001.

S: The news media have been magnificent, reporting around the clock tirelessly and efficiently to keep us up to the minute on all developments. As I knew, our armed forces are being prepared for war, with armed support from our many loyal allies. God bless them all.

Today there was a beautiful service at the National Cathedral. The president, members of his cabinet, world leaders and ministers of all denominations invoked our prayers for world peace. Praise God for blessing the world with great leaders.

Those who lost loved ones are bravely getting on with their lives. They feel they must set an example for the many parentless children who must grow up strong and brave. The country is offering moral and financial support, but even that seems so little in the overall tragedy. We can never bring back all those innocent ones who lost their lives.

Richard: Realize that, and give thanks for all your blessings, and do the very best you can in life to make the world a better place. Don't feel guilty because you fared better in these times. All of you face good times and bad. Deal with them sensibly and courageously, and thank God for His bounty.

◆   ◆   ◆

September 21, 2001.

S: The president's speech last night strengthened our resolves for a positive outcome of this war on evil, and for imminent peace.

Edelweiss: For those of you grieving and anxious about your loved ones who perished, be comforted. Your people are here, closely attended by angels. They are adjusting, and are only concerned about and praying for their bereaved ones left behind to grieve. They want you to deal with your sorrow positively and go on with your lives. They will be fine, and you will be reunited one day.

S: What about those suicide pilots?

Edelweiss: We can't tell you all, but they are not happy. Their picture of life in Paradise in the arms of Allah just didn't gel.

S: Good. They must learn what monstrous things they did.

Edelweiss: Believe me, they will. The angels consoling and counseling the new arrivals are elated and proud that they are so anxious to become working members of our Spirit world. Most of them want to be guides, to comfort and protect their loved ones from their Spirit home. We don't know yet what garden they will live in, but they all want to stay together. This is understandable and will be granted.

S: God bless and keep them. They are so special. Please pray, my angels, that no more of these horrible things will occur.

Edelweiss: There are some things we can inspire or prevent, but we cannot interfere with freedom of thought or action when such desperate fanaticism is involved. We want these fanatics to face justice on Earth, but be certain all those in Spirit will!

Richard: Your country is reacting in a most positive way. United and strong, compassionate and courageous are your people and those who lead them. We are proud of you and all your allies giving support.

Once again a powerful alliance has been united with the awakening of the Sleeping giant.

S: What does our friend Osama bin Laden think now of our awakened Giant? Where is he?

Richard: Hiding. He is so scared now he wants to get out of Afghanistan. He won't have many supporters in his flight to safer ground now that he is targeted. However, there is one who for political reason and for vengeance wants to help him and to join forces with him to plot future evil. Saddam Hussein. Don't be surprised is Saddam manages to sneak him into Iraq. It's not probable, but it's possible. The world will not be a safe place to live until both are eliminated.

S: Bin Laden has a 10-year-old son, whom he has taught violence and hatred of all strength and decency.

Richard: He will share his father's fate. Poor kid. He will not be held responsible in Spirit, and will learn a whole new picture of life—kindness, friends, education, cleanliness, beautiful surroundings, adorable pets, even *fun*!

S: It's a shame he couldn't have all that on Earth.

Richard: Just another example of the contagion of terrorism. These fanatics are sadistic animals. Look how they treat their women. Muslim women are honest, hardworking and intelligent. If given their rights, they would be an asset to world economy, politics and society as so many women in the free world have been. Bin Laden says he is acting in the Name of Allah. Allah will give him a kick in the behind.

Your government is very angry, and when the Giant is provoked, look out. No more Mr. Nice Guy Uncle Sam!

You have the support not only of all the decent world—powerful both politically and militarily—but also of your Spirit "armies." This is the time to end terrorism. Let's get 'em!

Notes

While not quoted directly, several resources helped me in the preparation of this book among them:

The New Grove Dictionary of Music and Musicians, Vol. 18 (1980);

The World of Music Illustrated Encyclopedia (1963);

The Harper Dictionary of Opera and Operetta (James Anderson, 1989);

The Metropolitan Opera Encyclopedia (Ed. David Hamilton);

Encyclopedia of the Third Reich (Dr. Louis L. Snyder, 1976);

Recording synopses:

"You Are My Heart's Delight," Tony Watts, 1994

"My Love For You" Peter Gammond, 1996.

0-595-22224-2

www.ingramcontent.com/pod-product-compliance
Lightning Source LLC
Chambersburg PA
CBHW020248290526
45784CB00003B/1144